Dieter Roelstraete

Fredrik Værslev: World Paintings

Mousse Publishing

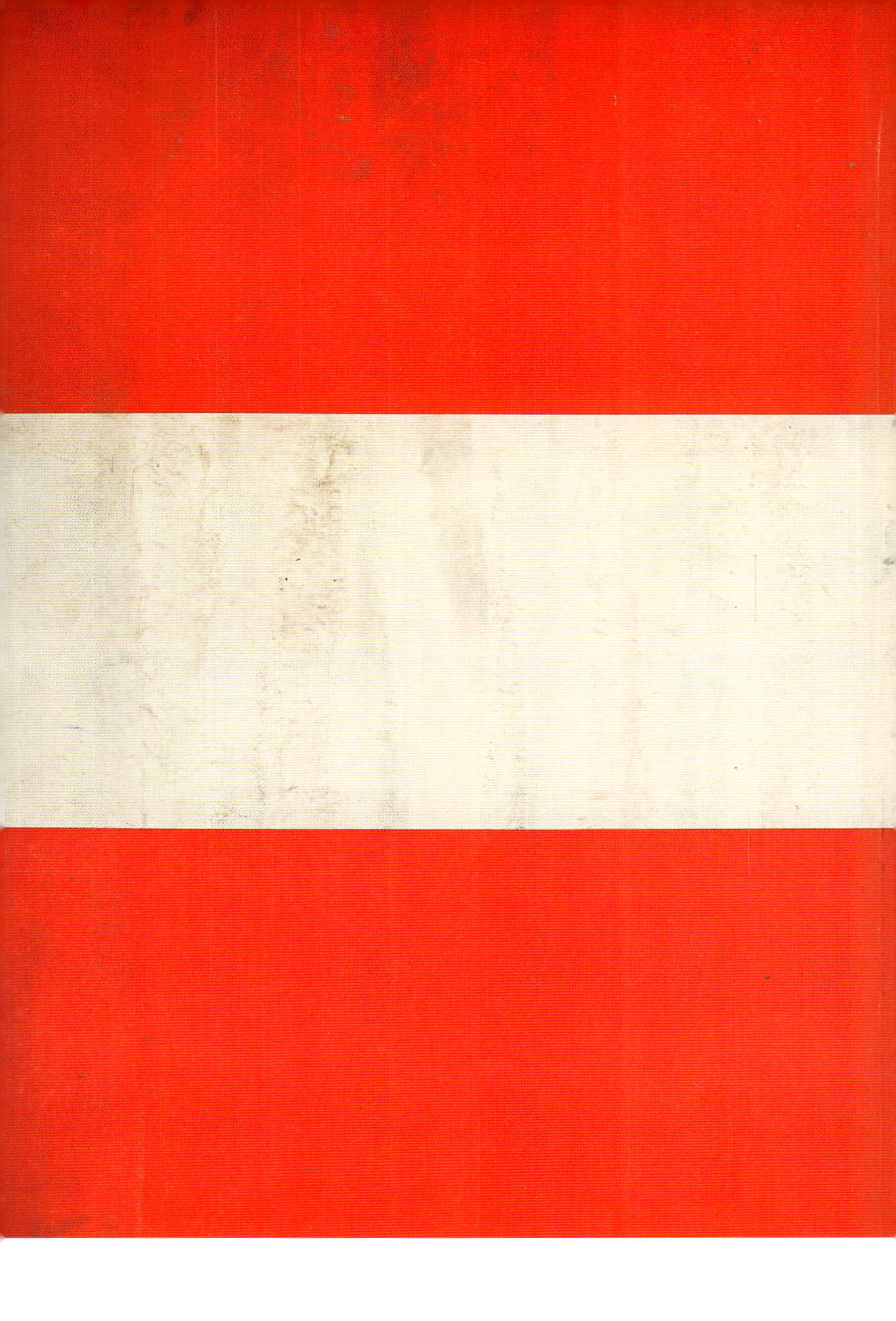

AUSTRIA

P 2

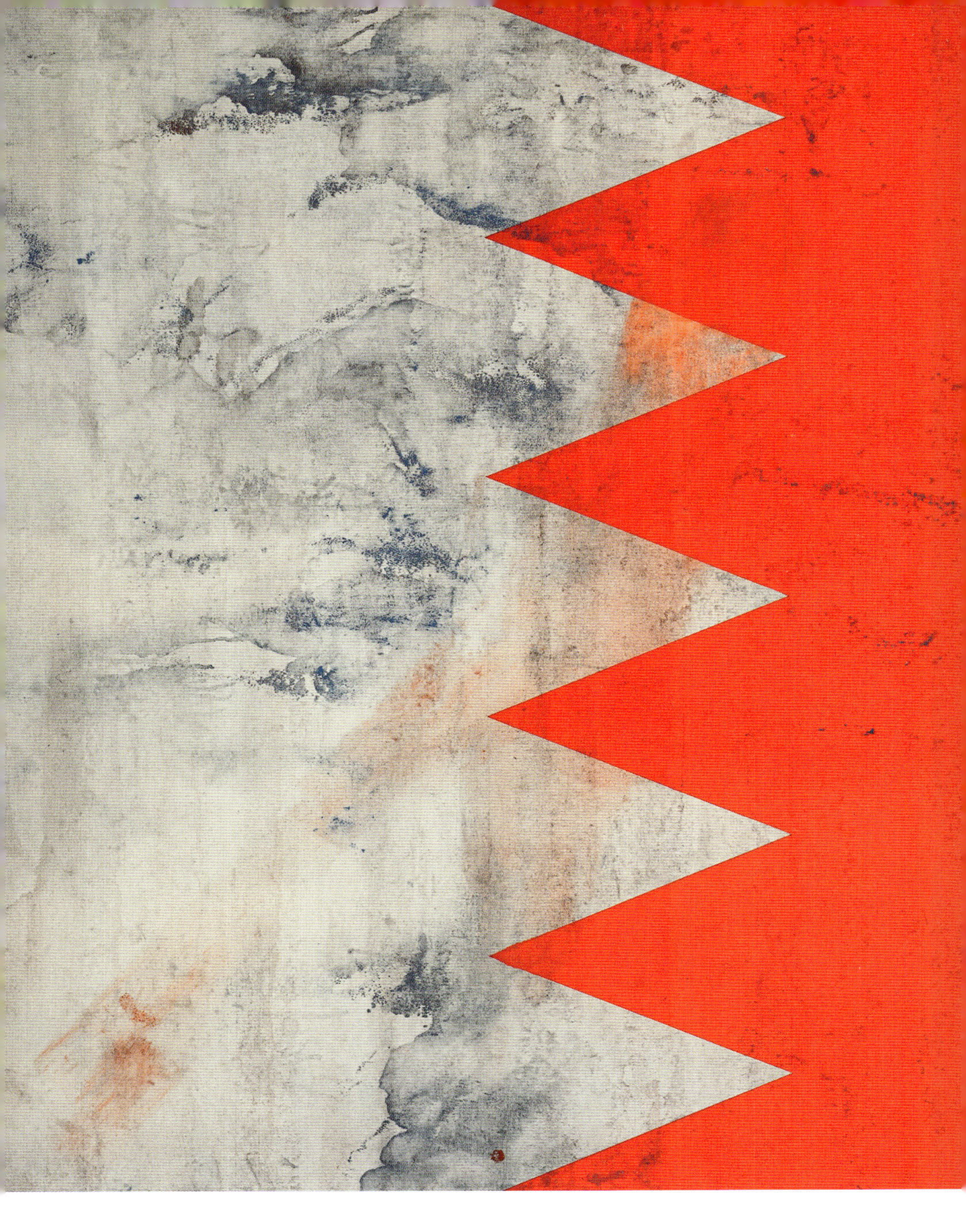

BAHRAIN

P 4

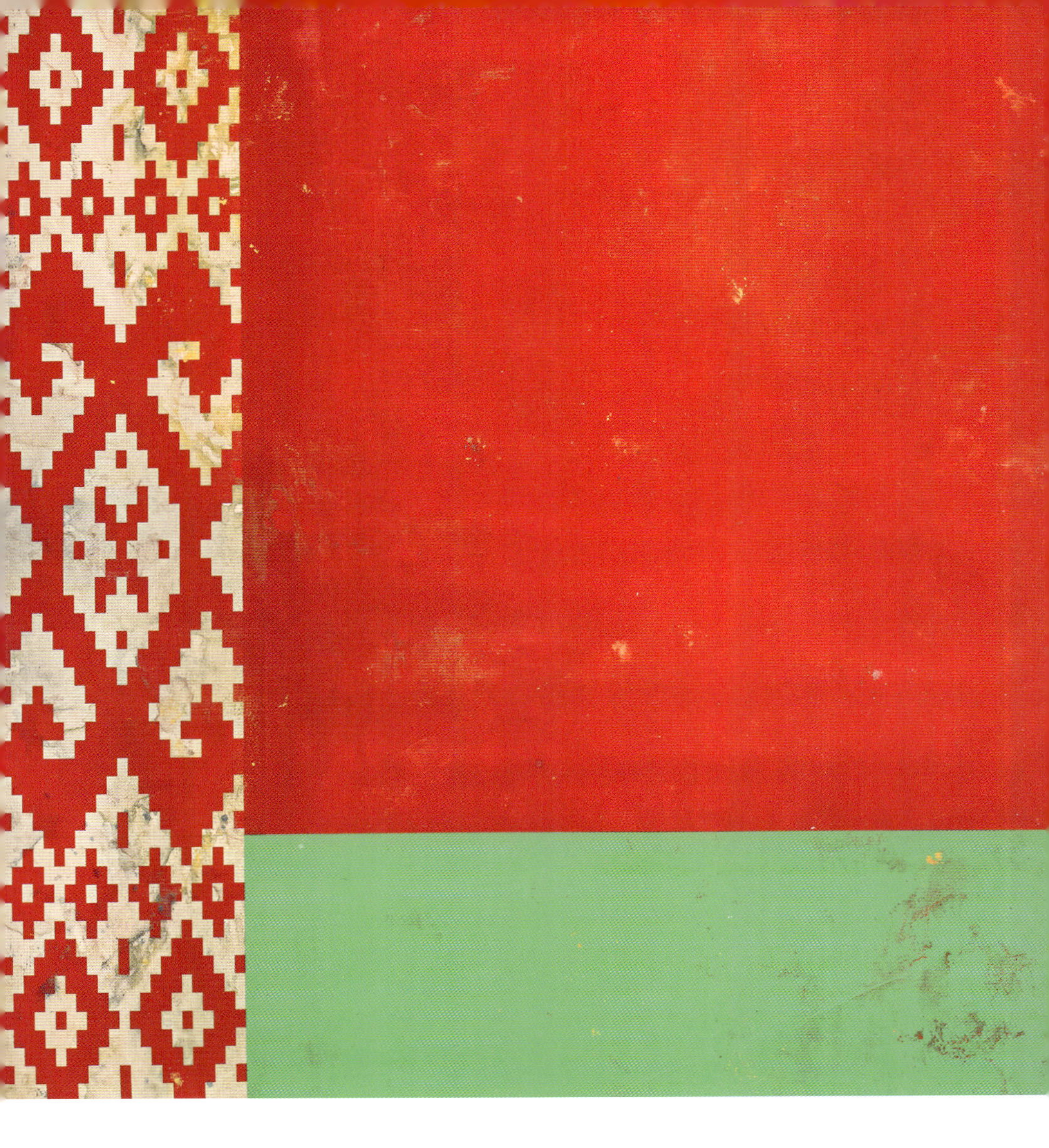

BELARUS

P 6

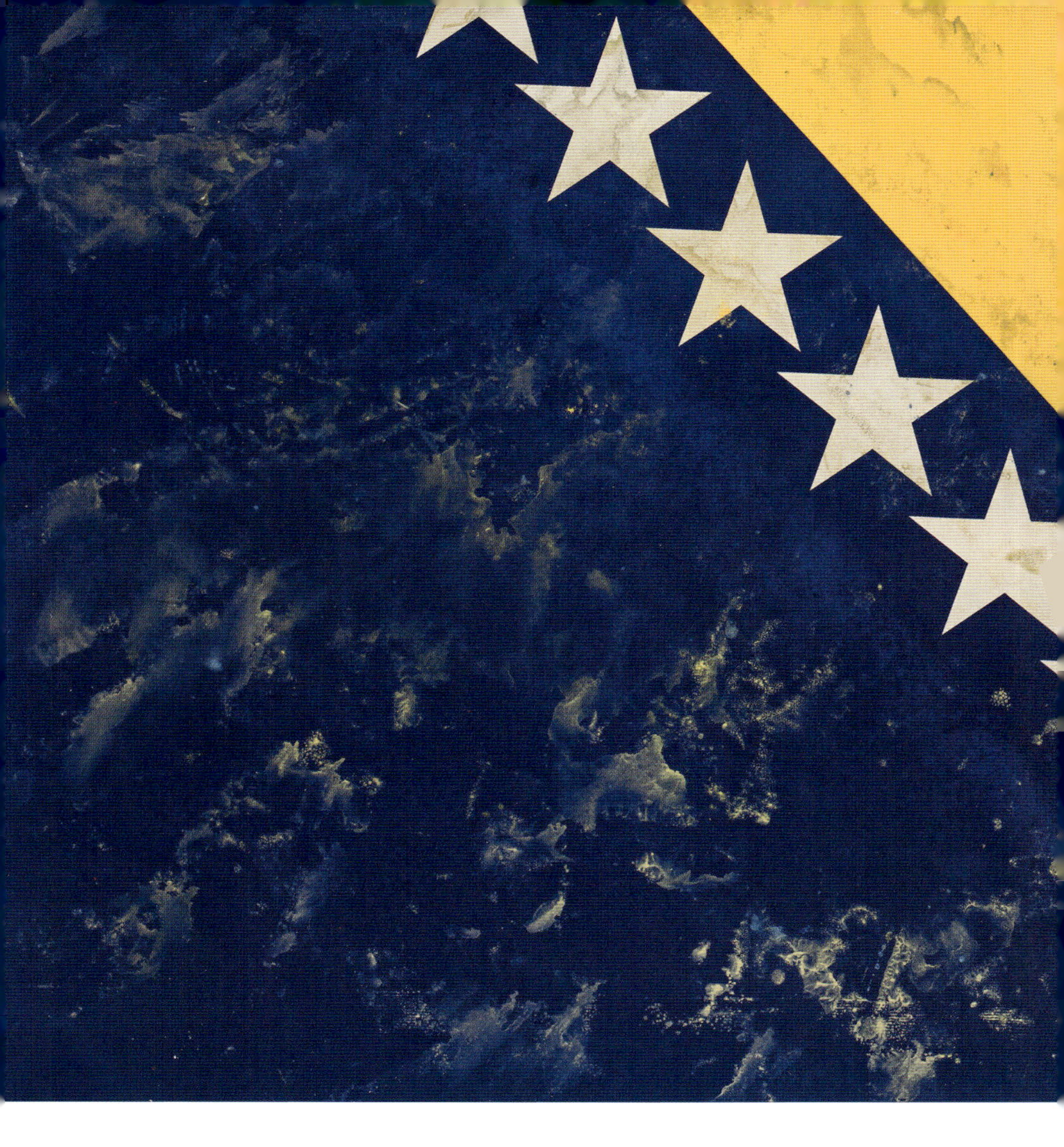

BOSNIA AND HERZEGOVINA

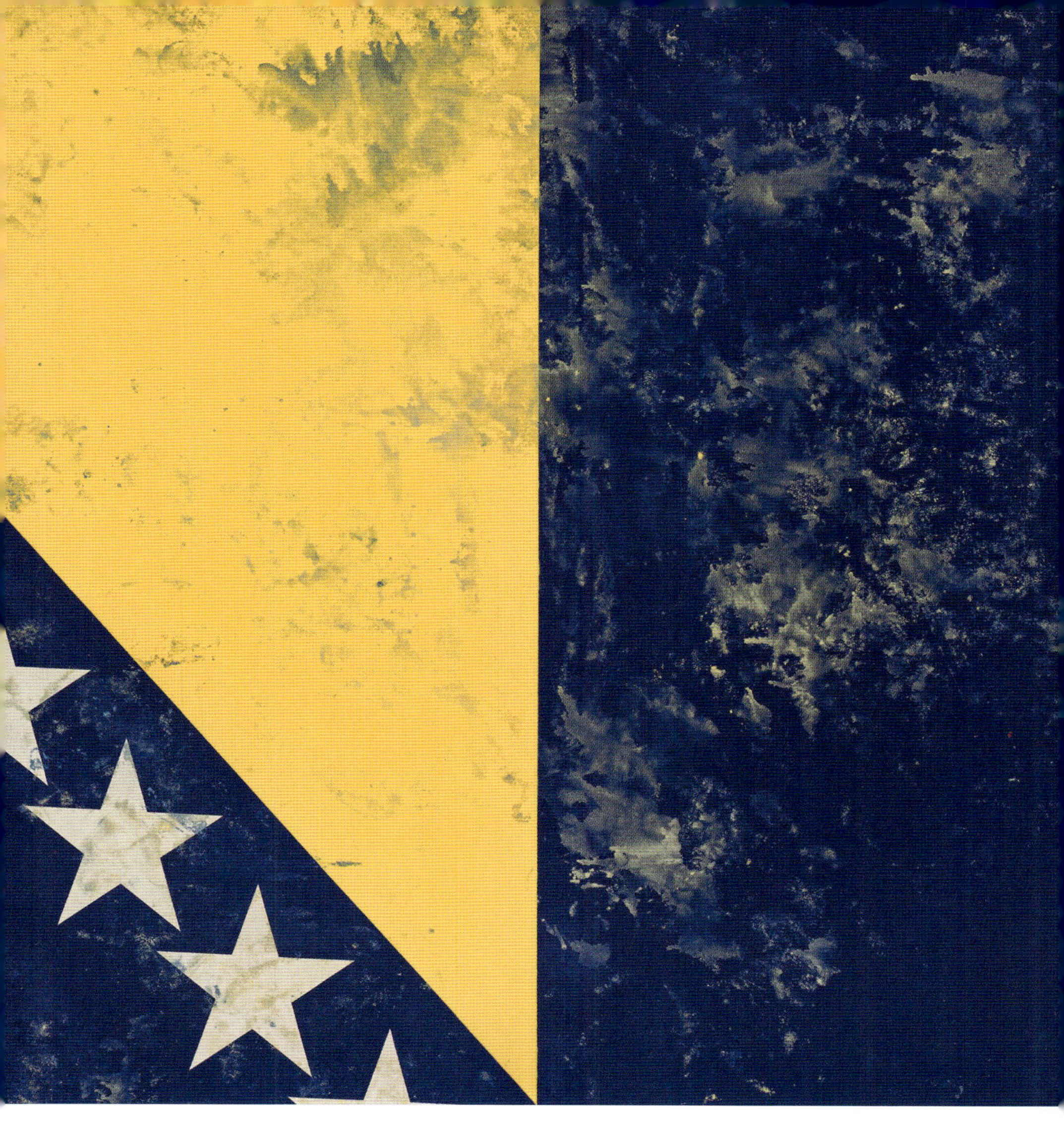

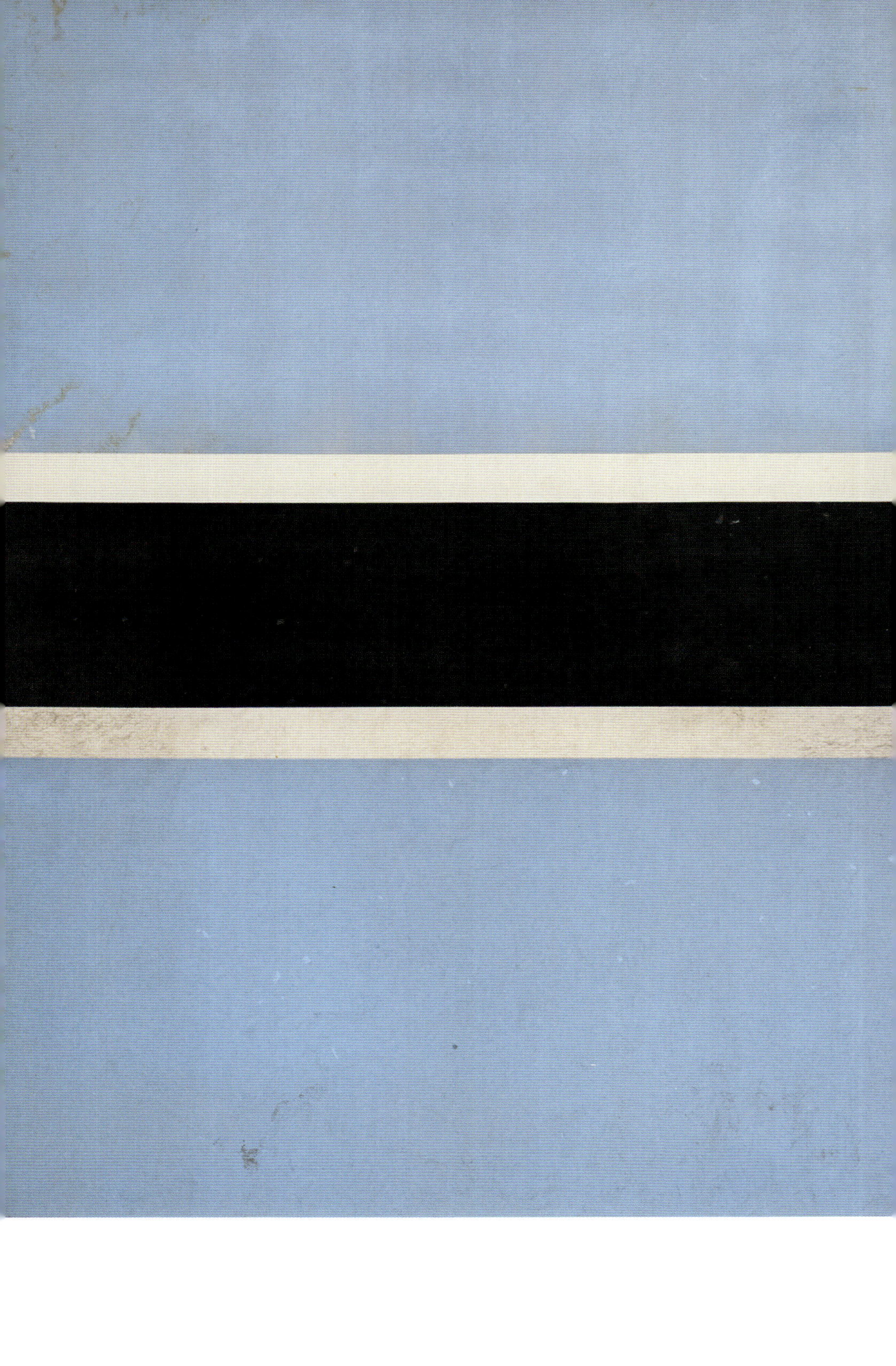

BOTSWANA

P 10

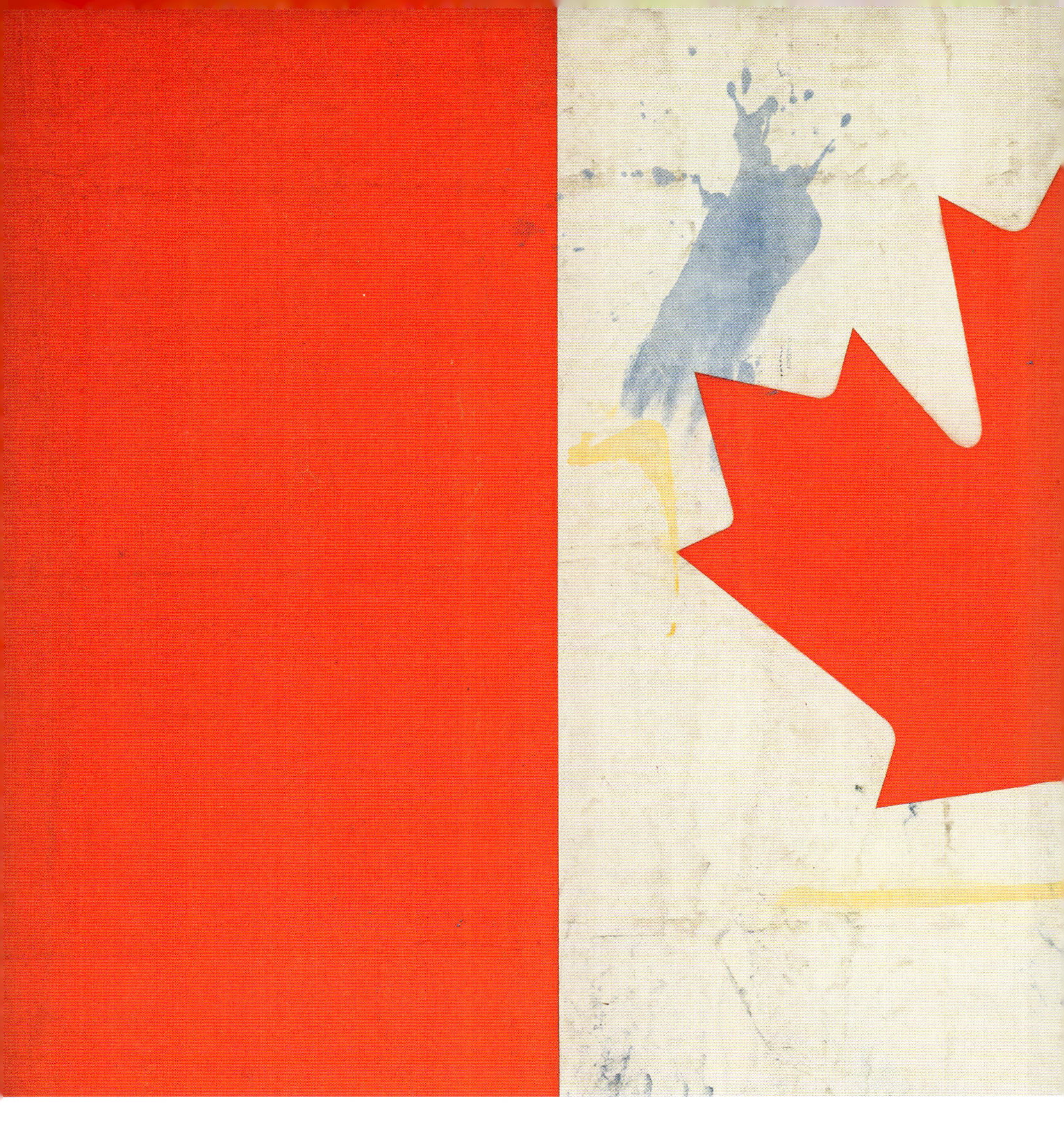

CANADA

P 12

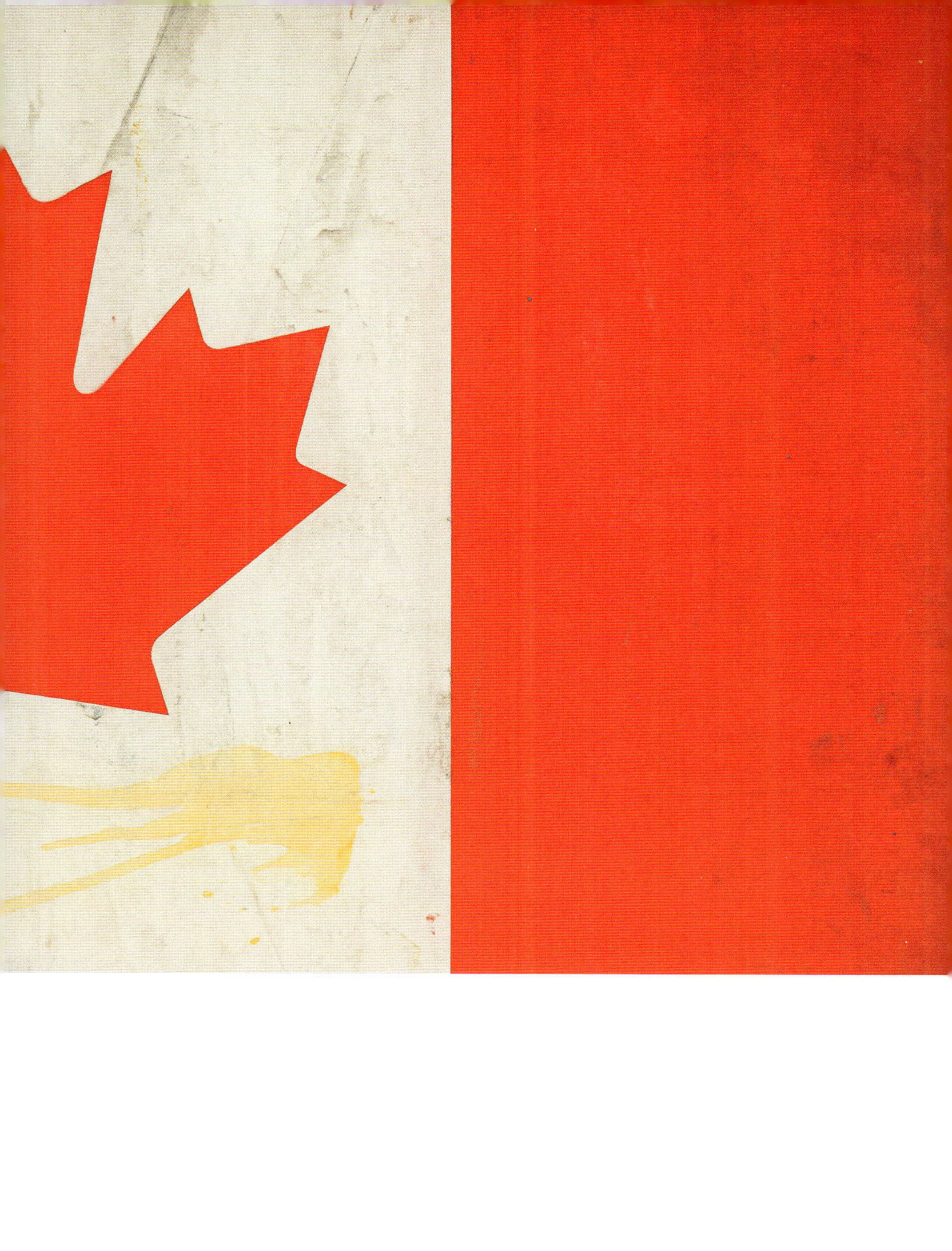

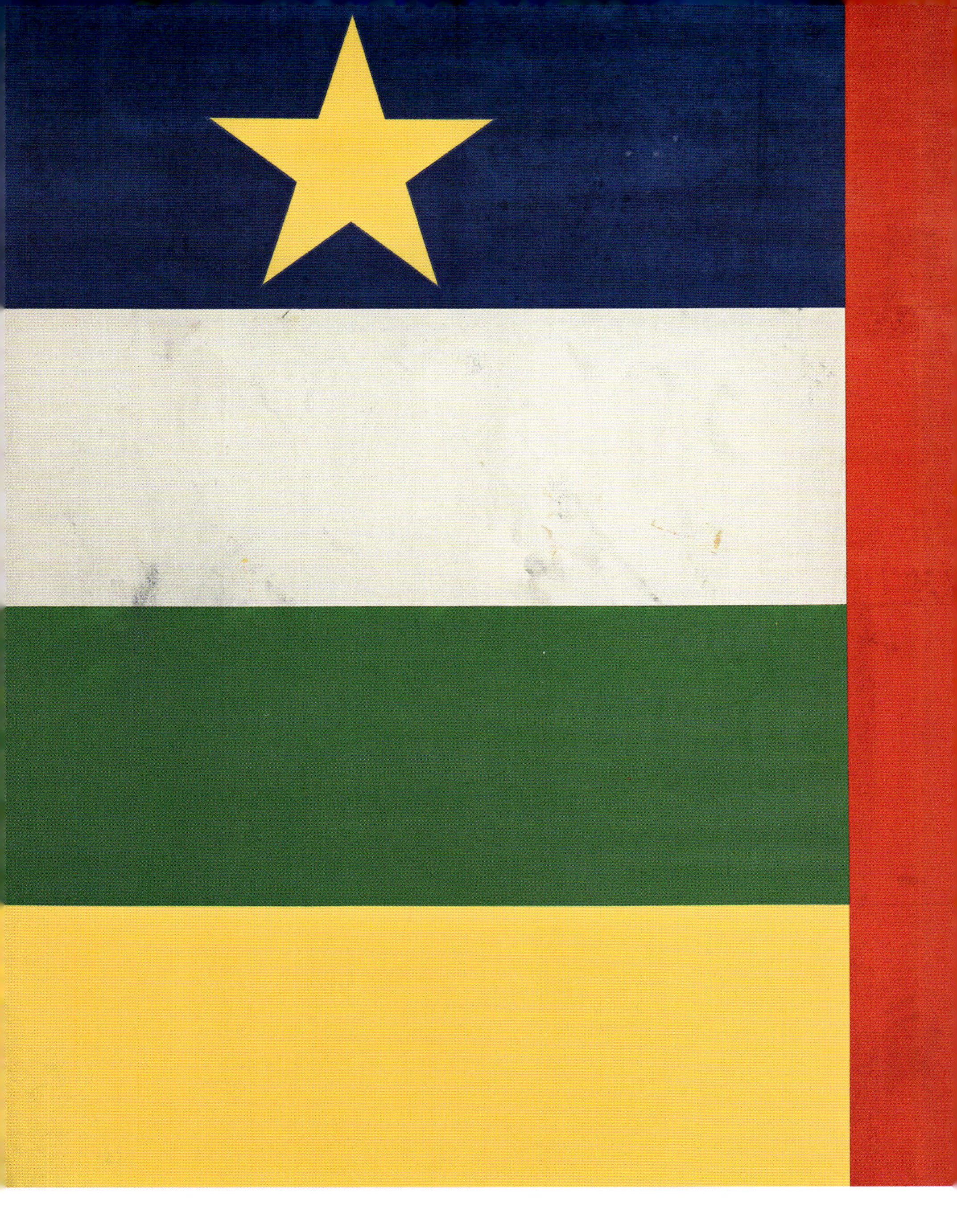

CENTRAL AFRICAN REPUBLIC

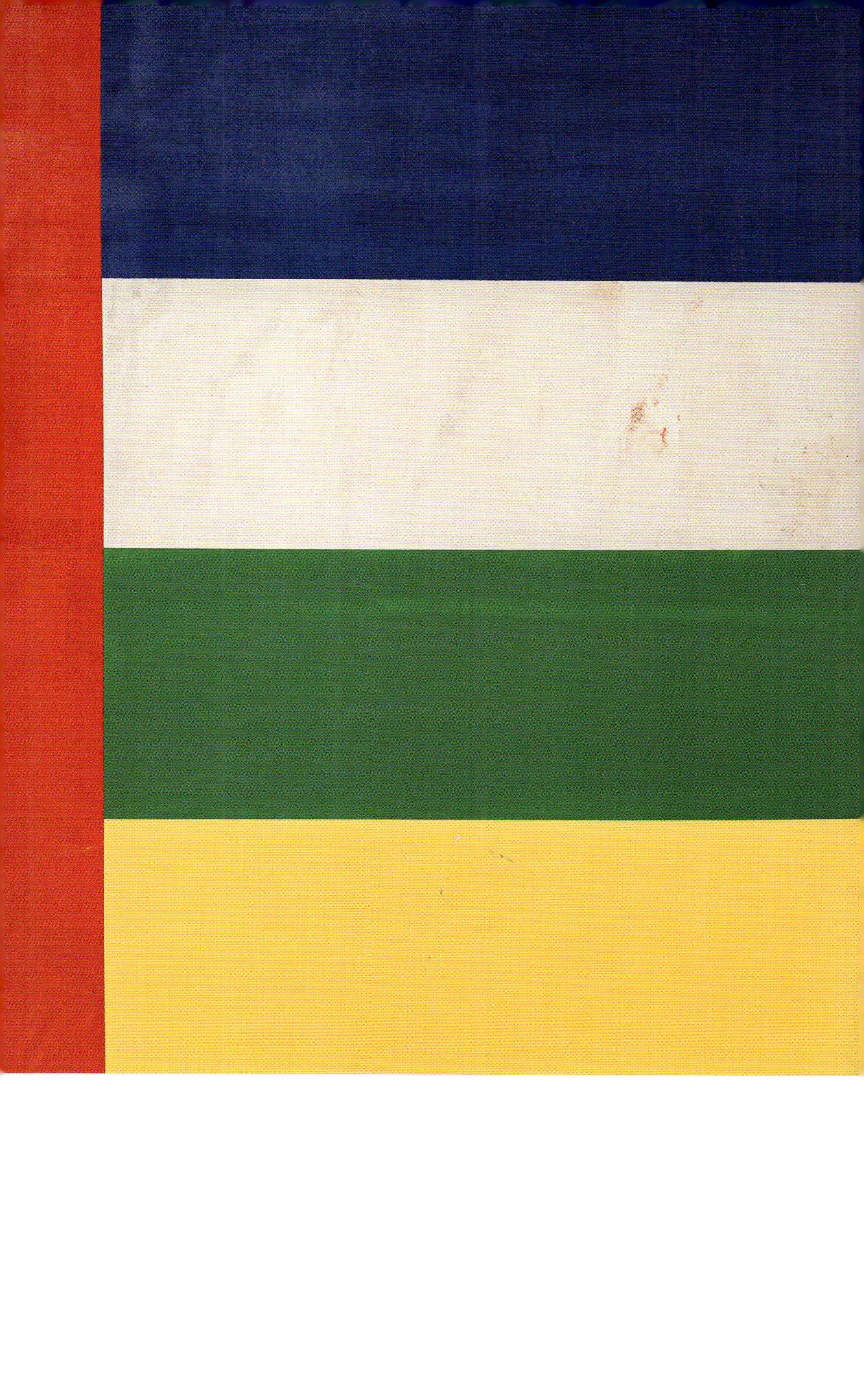

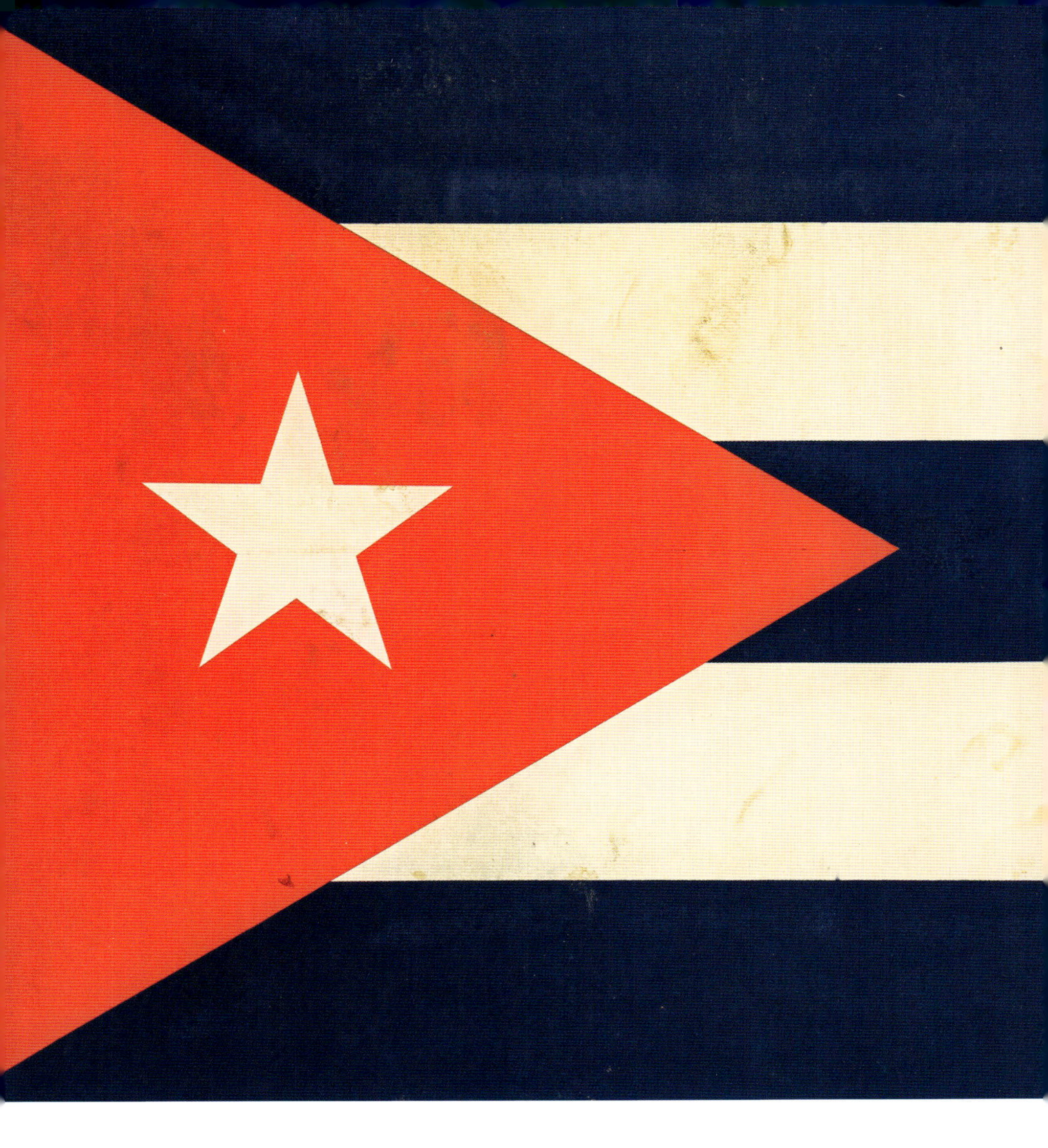

CUBA

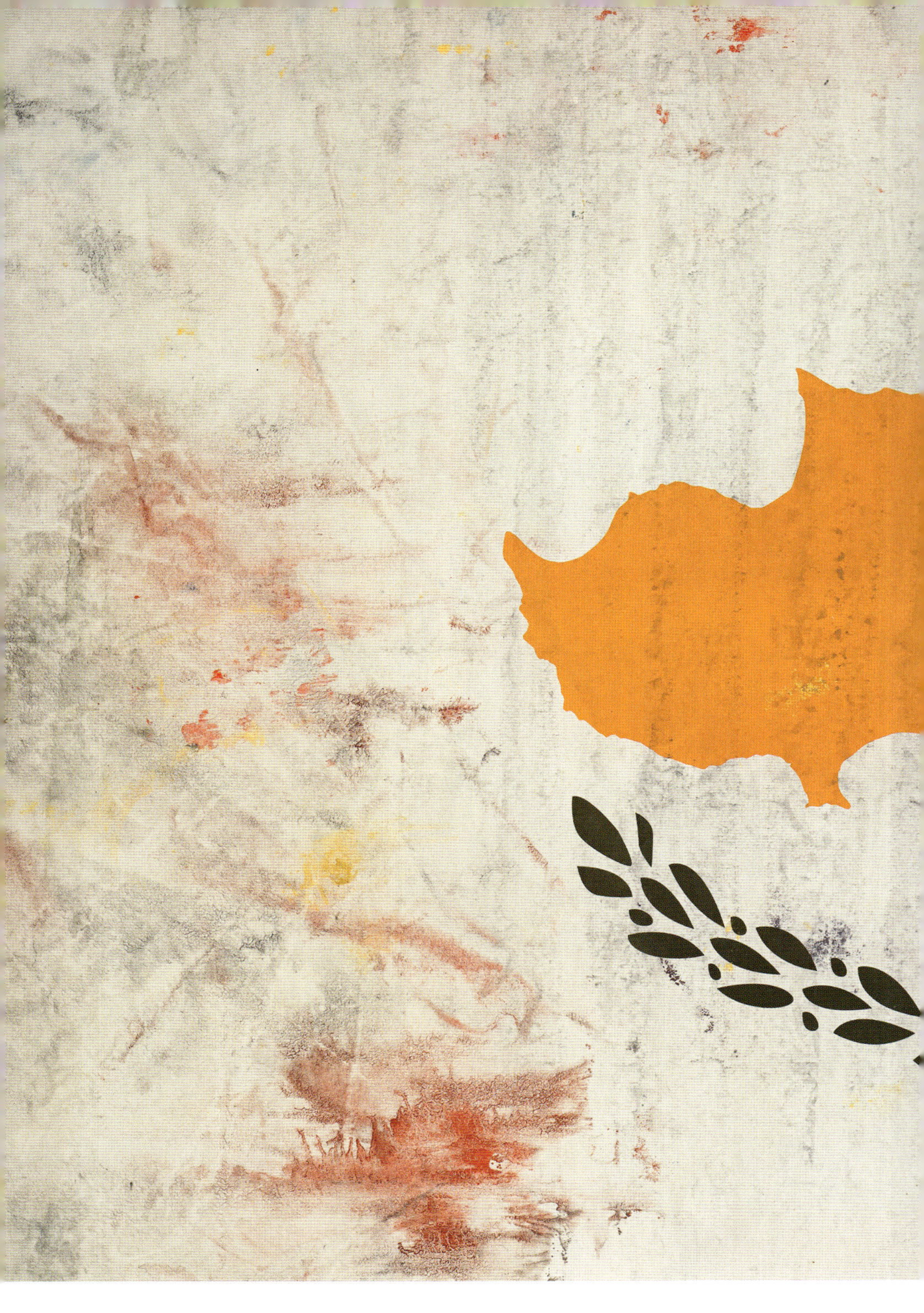

CYPRUS

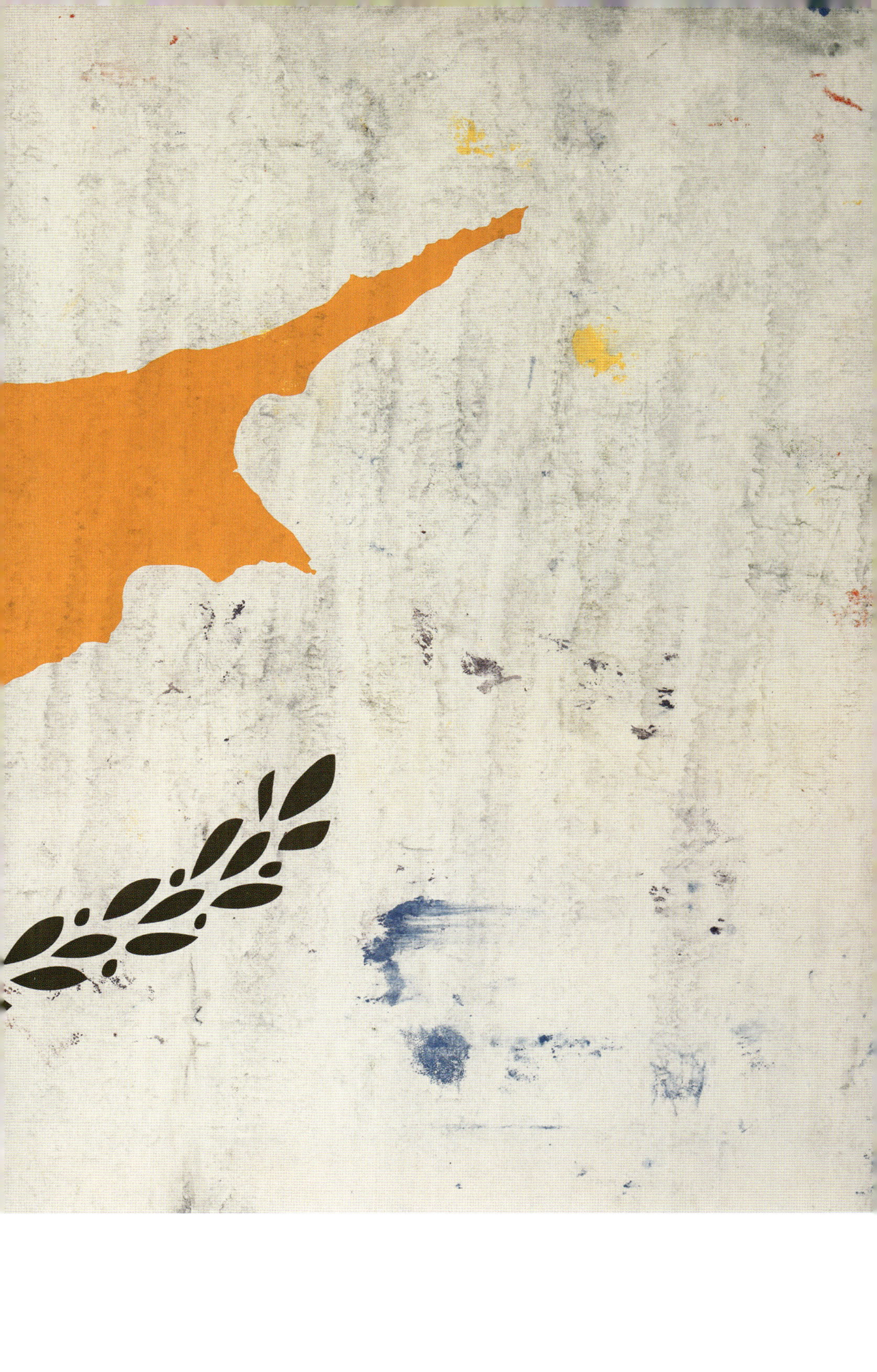

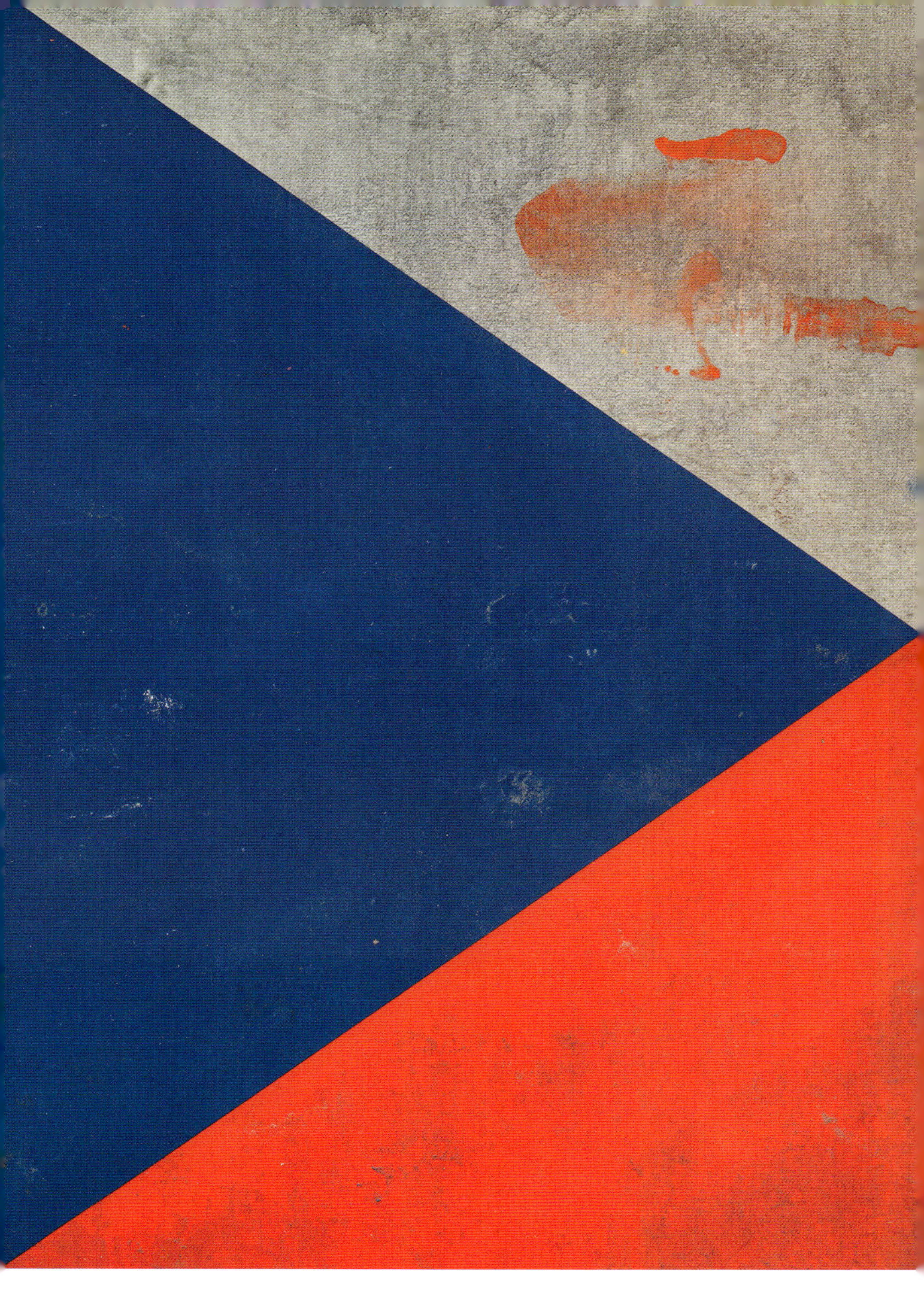

CZECH REPUBLIC

P 20

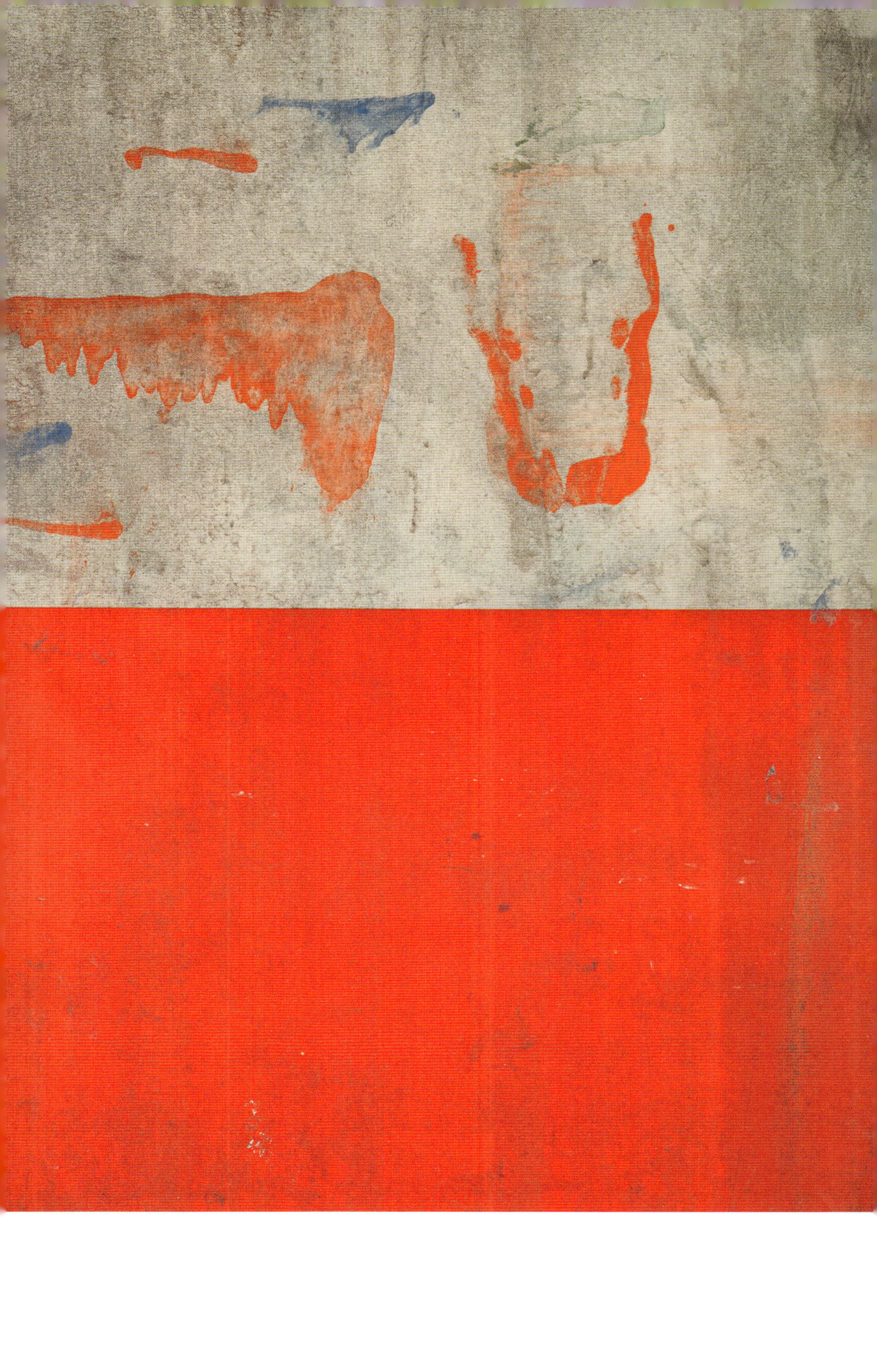

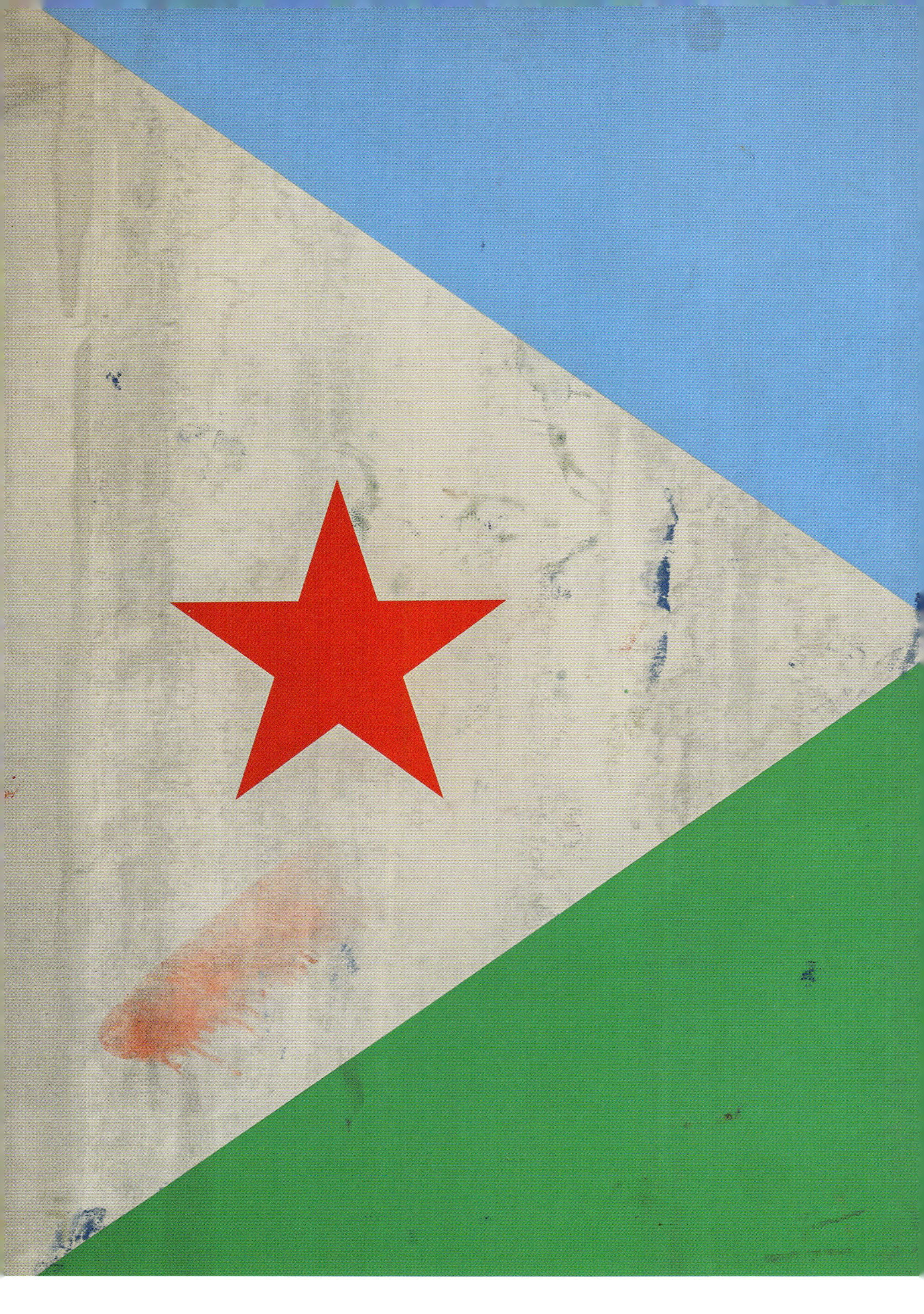

DJIBOUTI

P 22

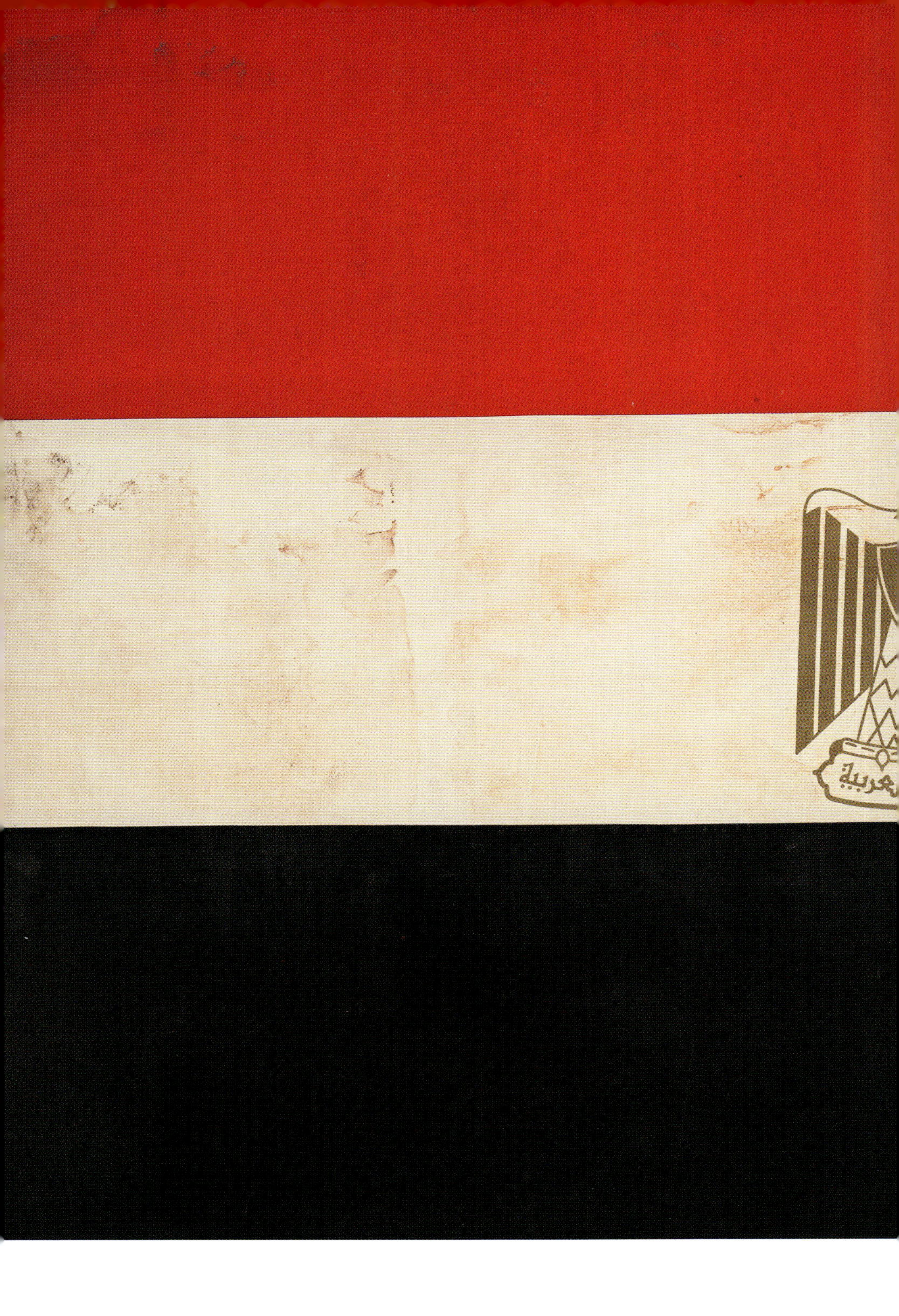

EGYPT

P 24

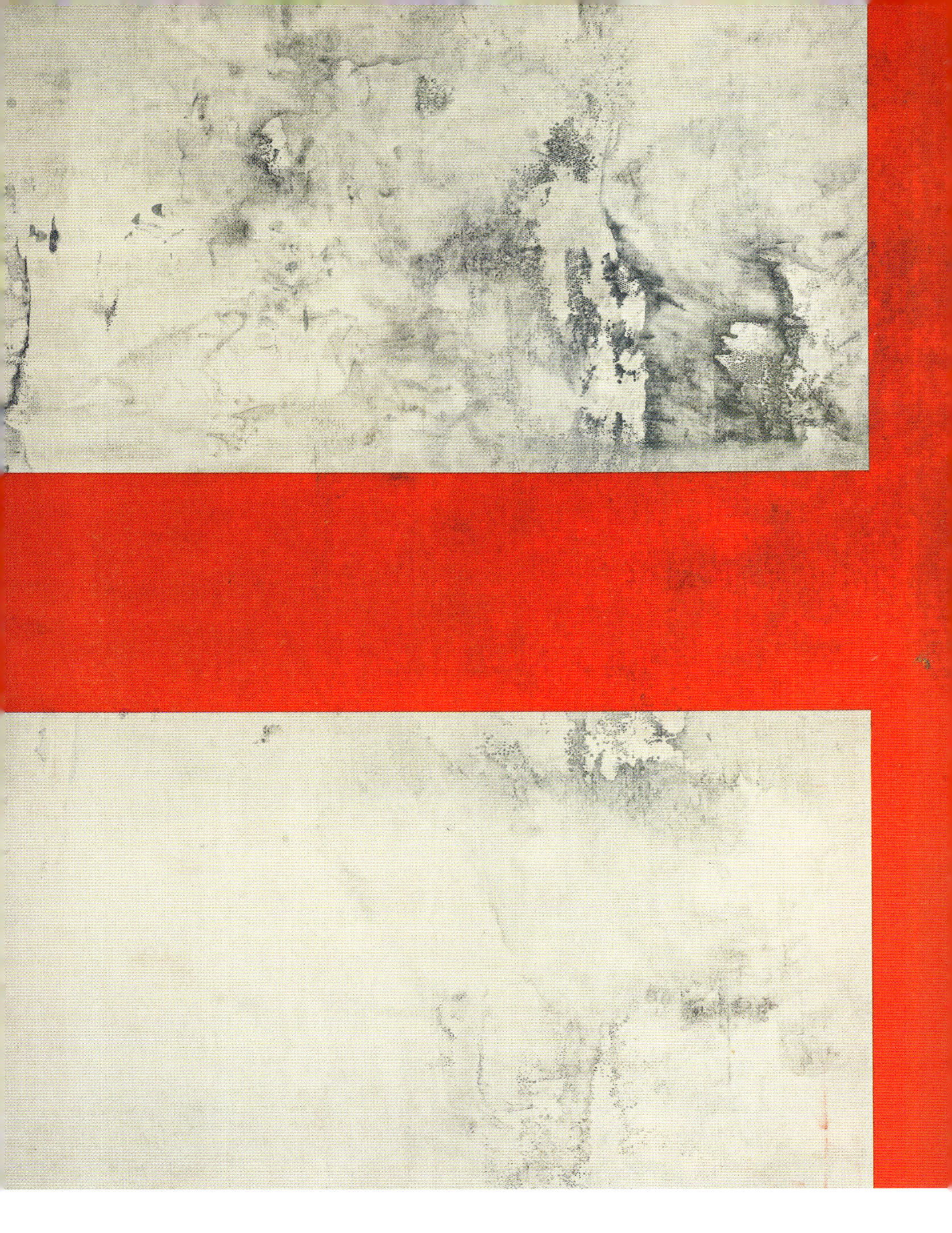

ENGLAND

P 26

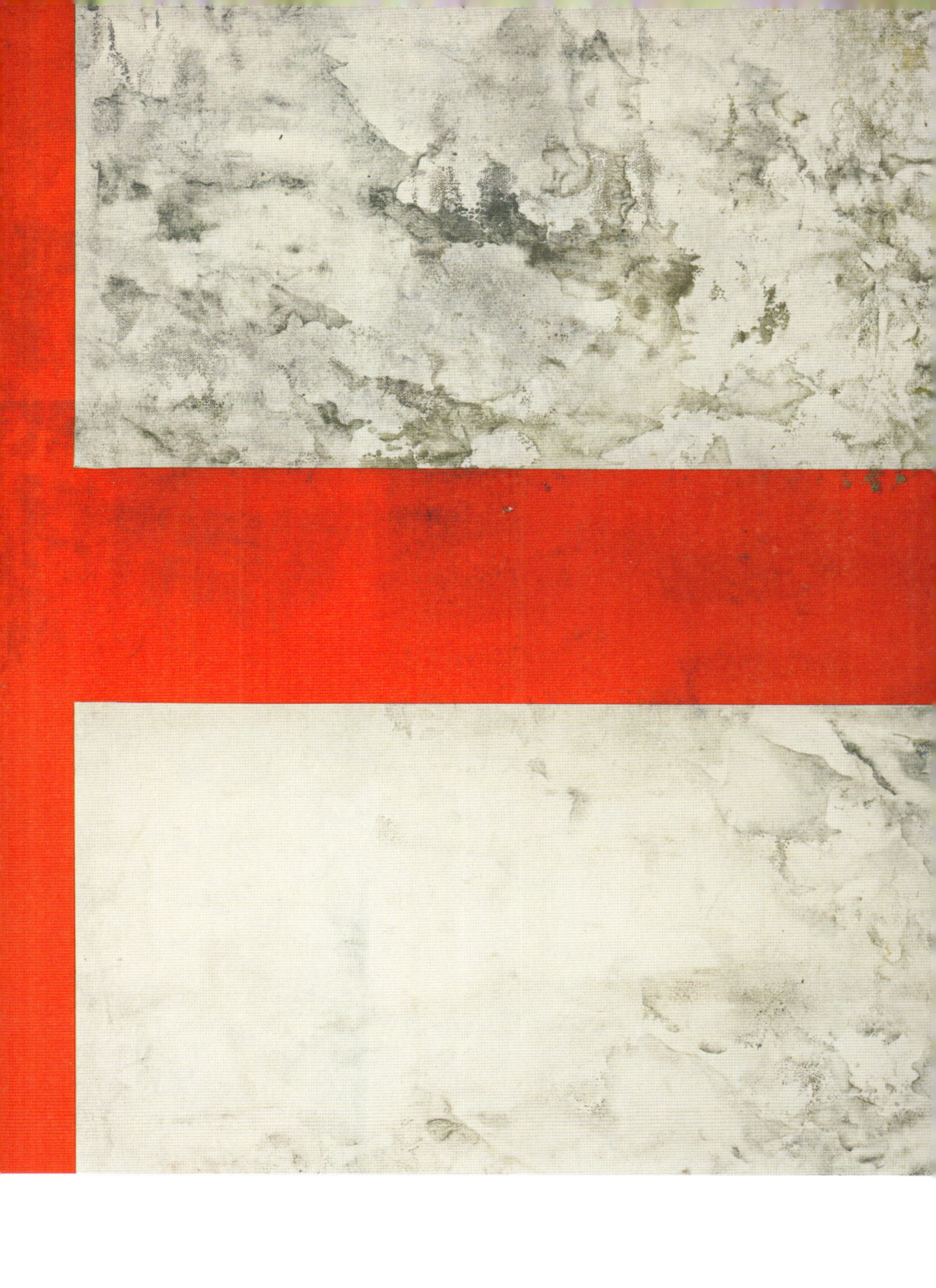

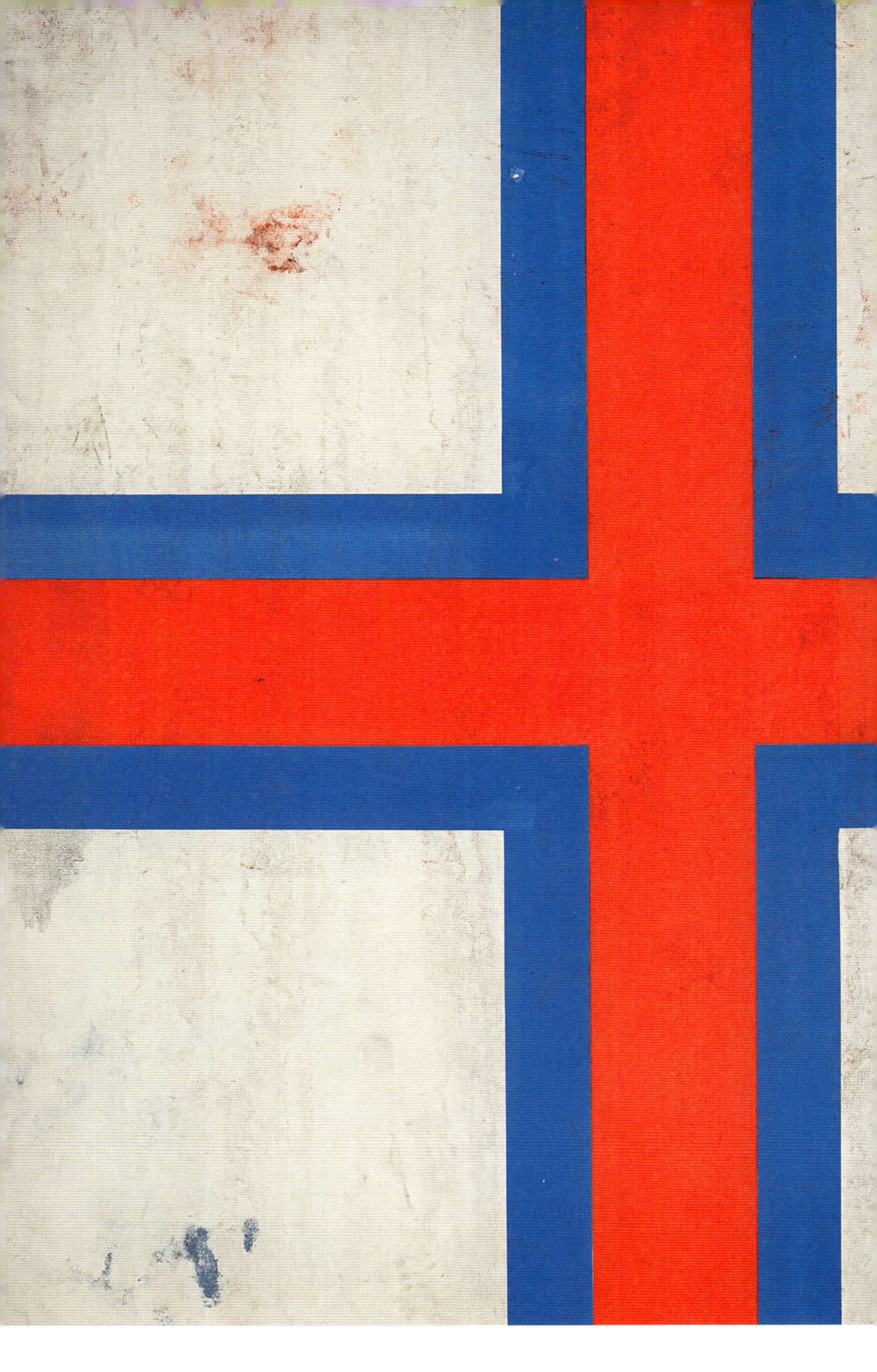

FAROE ISLANDS

P 28

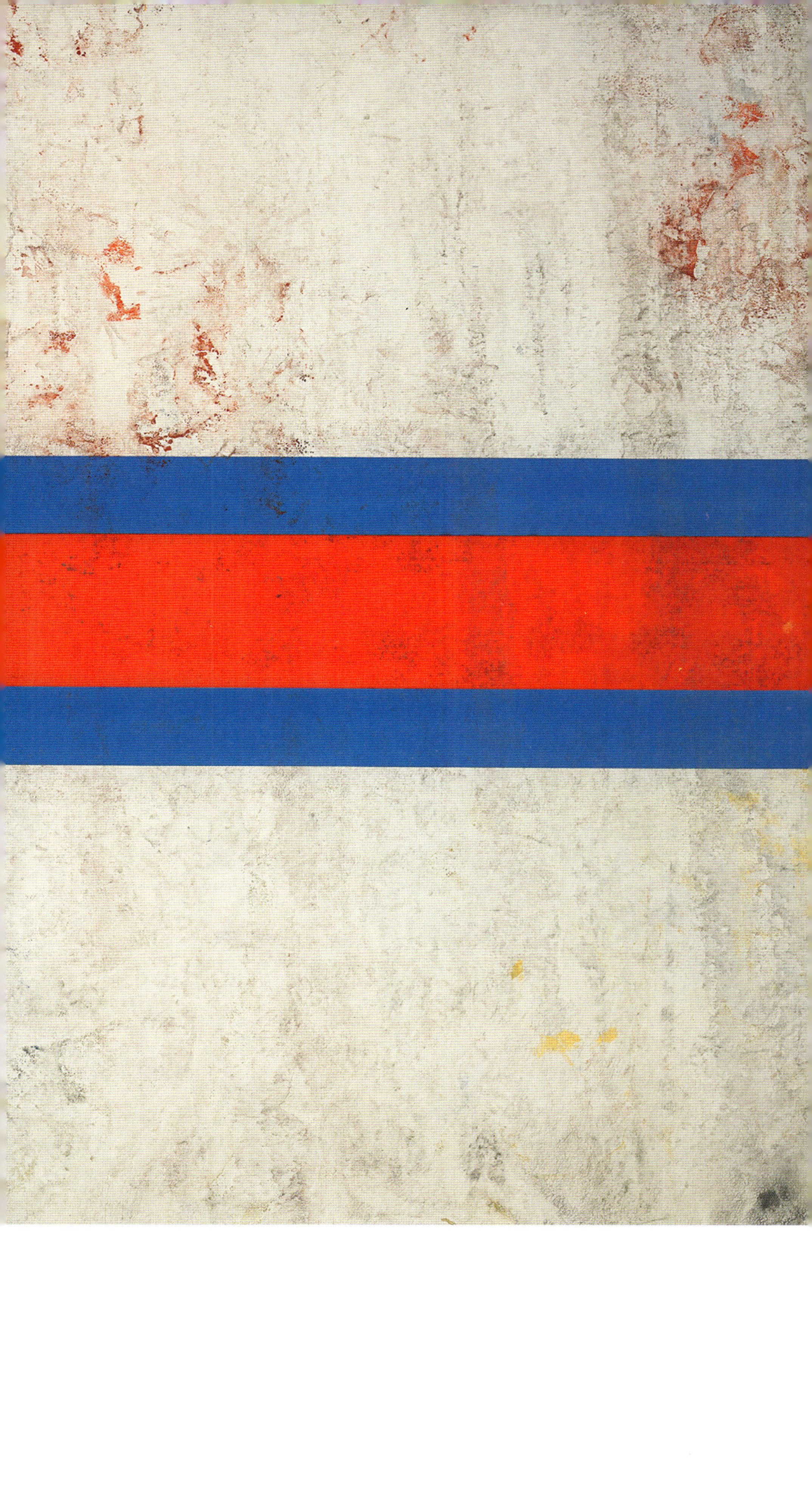

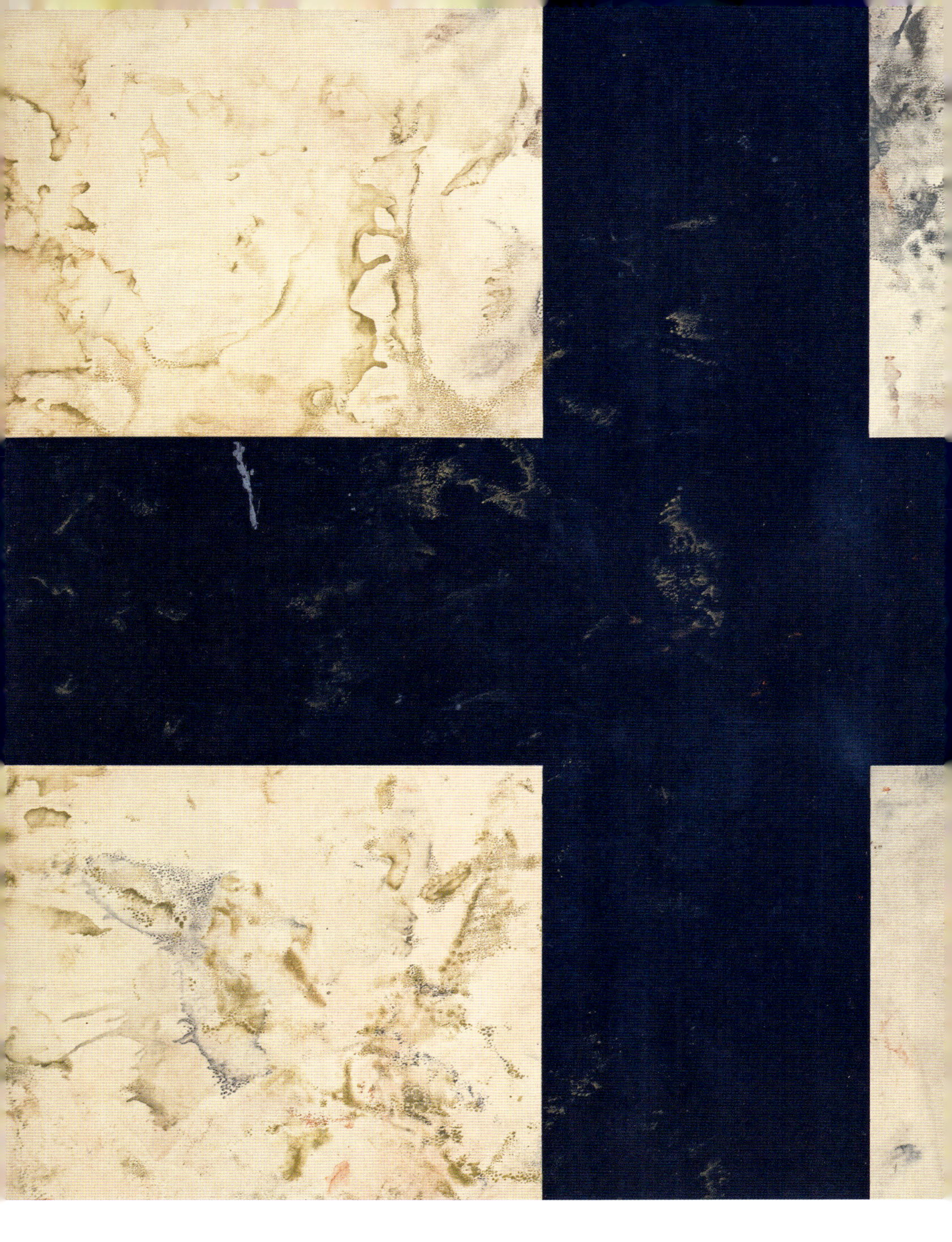

FINLAND

P 30

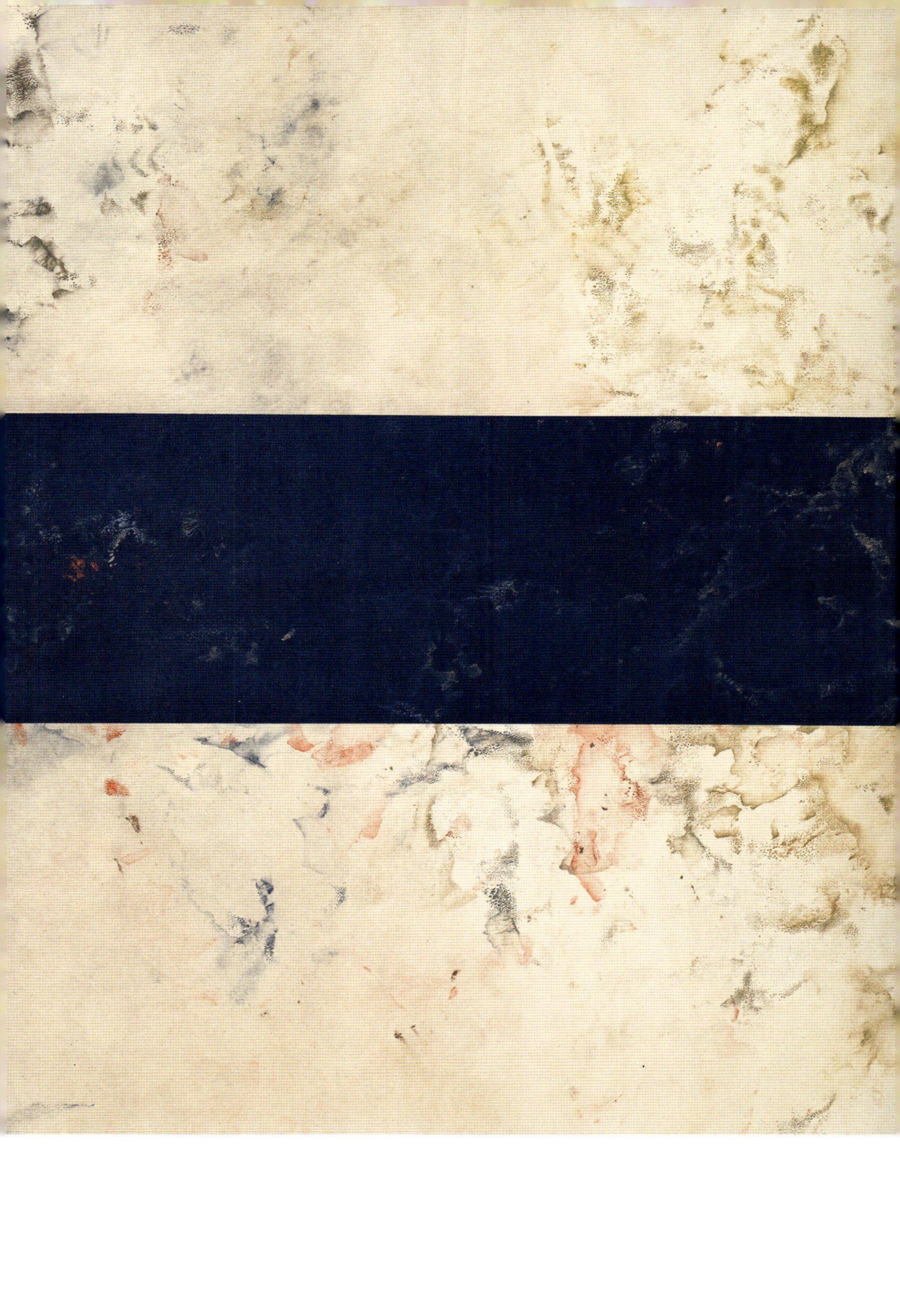

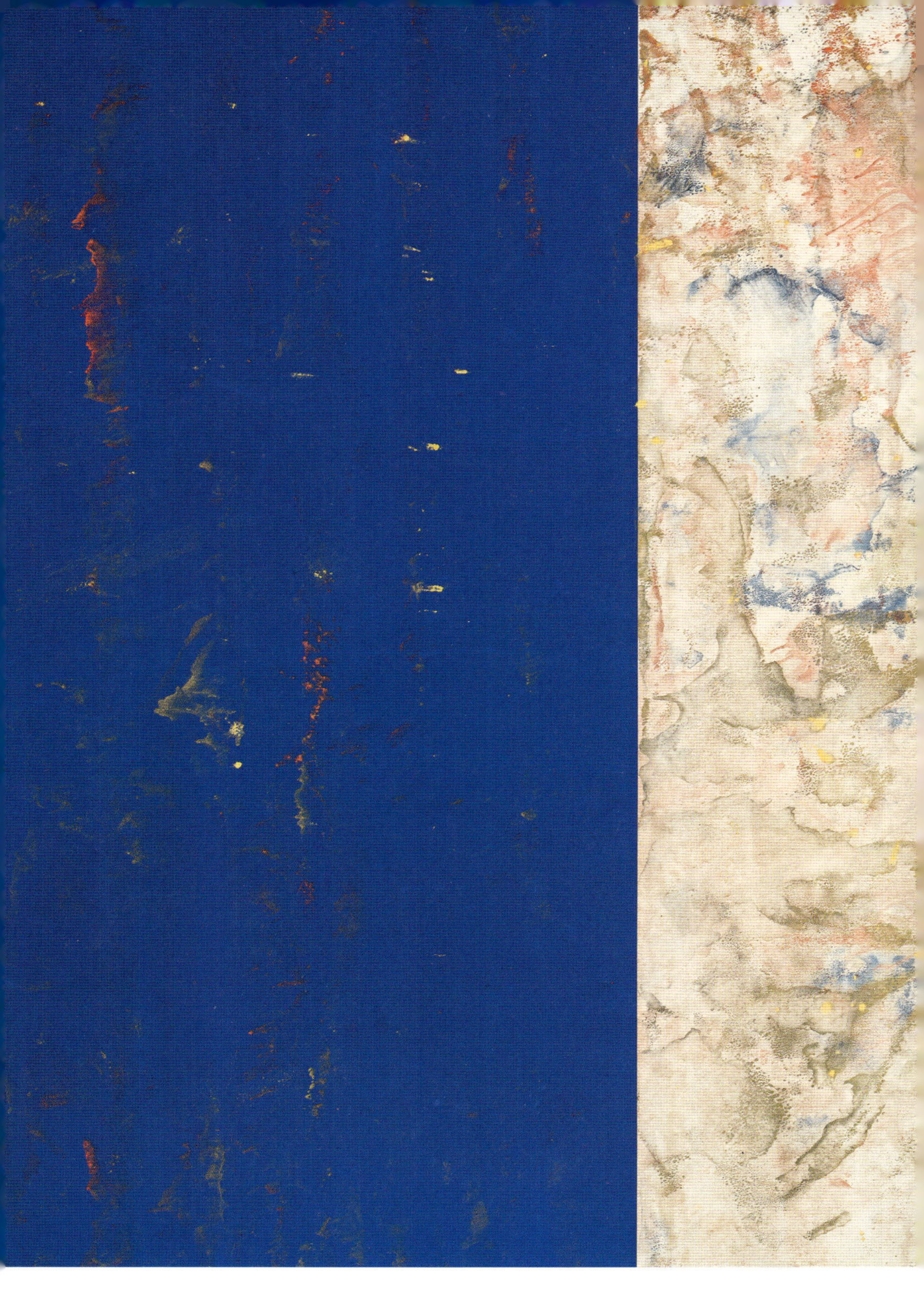

FRANCE

P 32

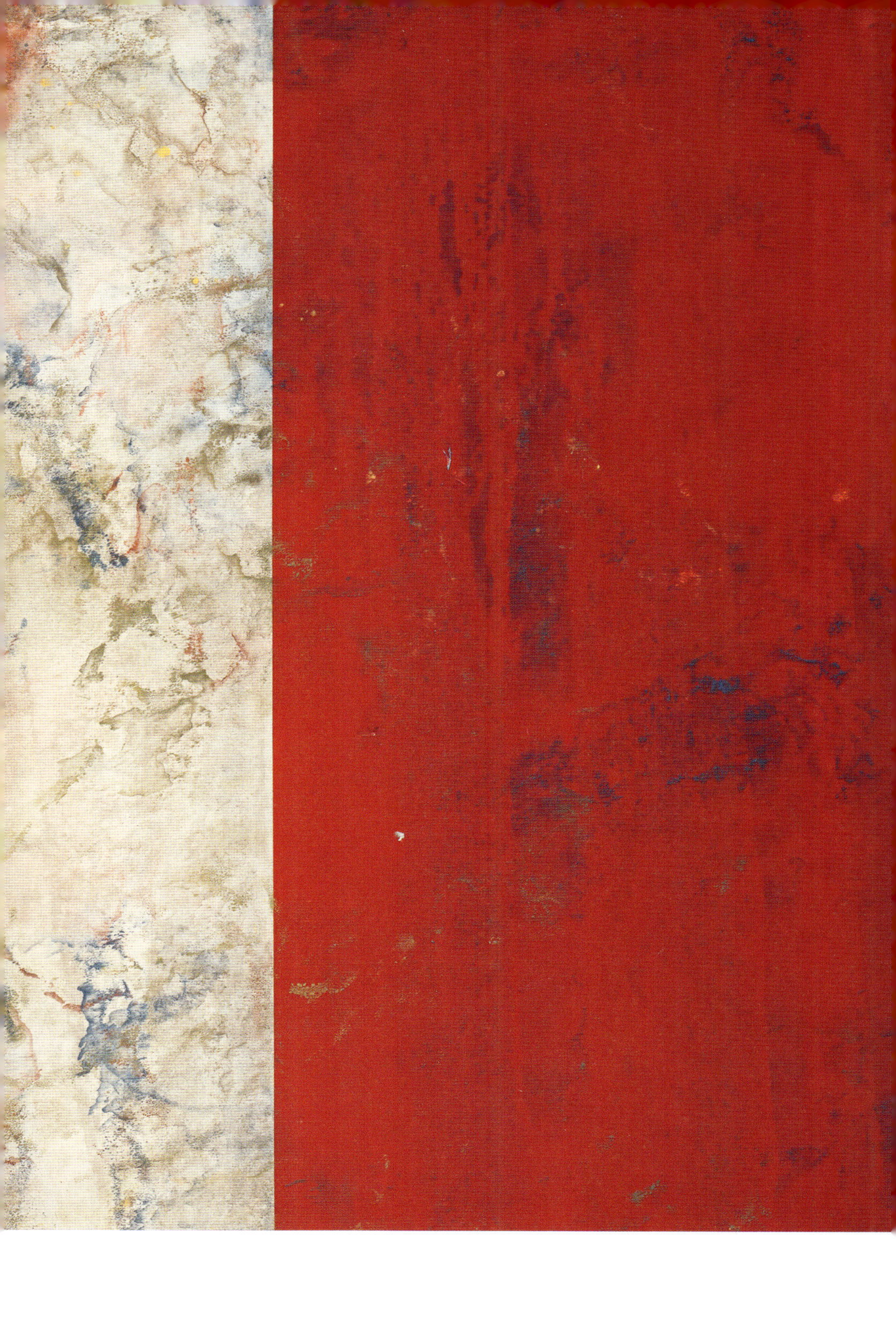

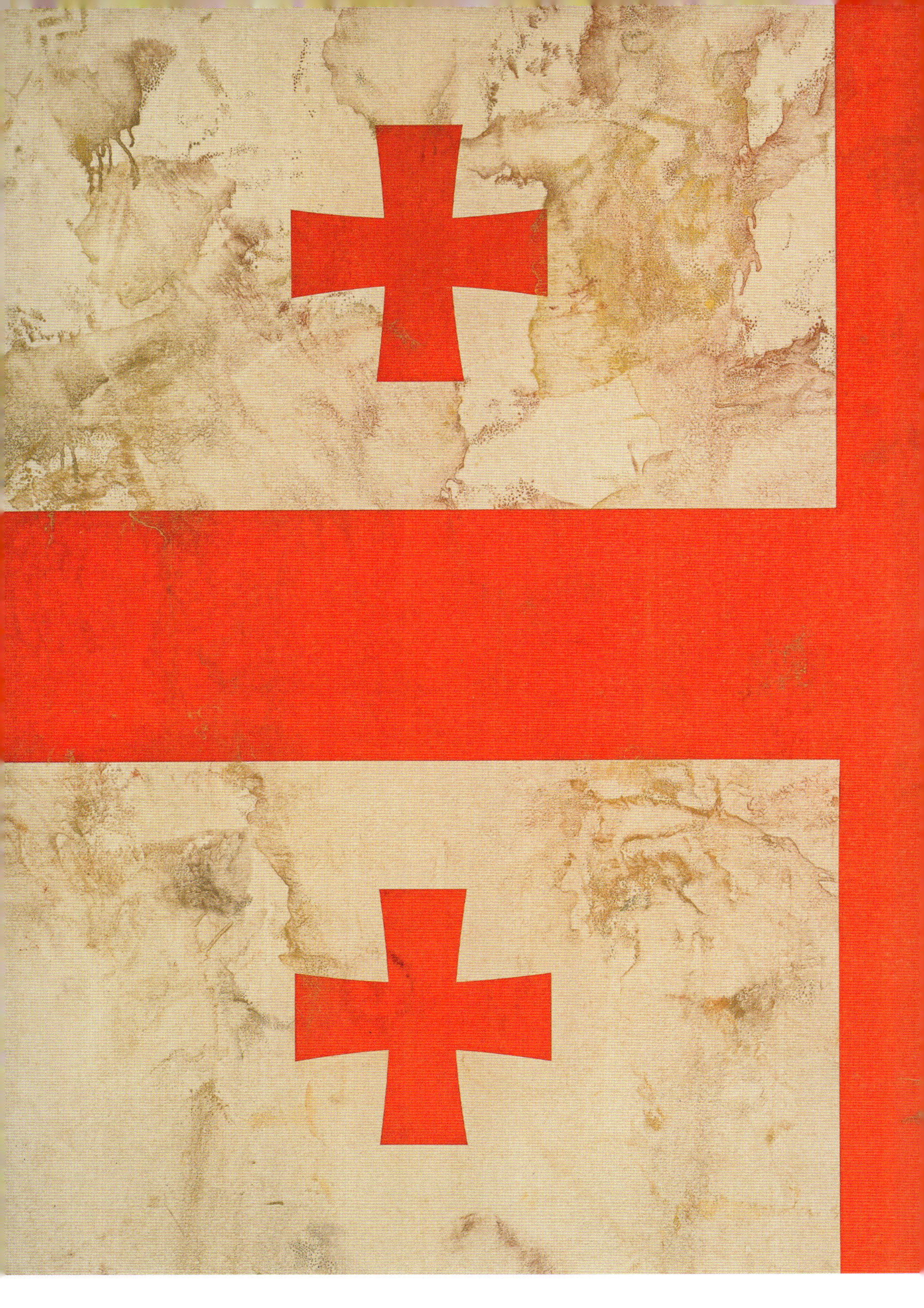

GEORGIA

P 34

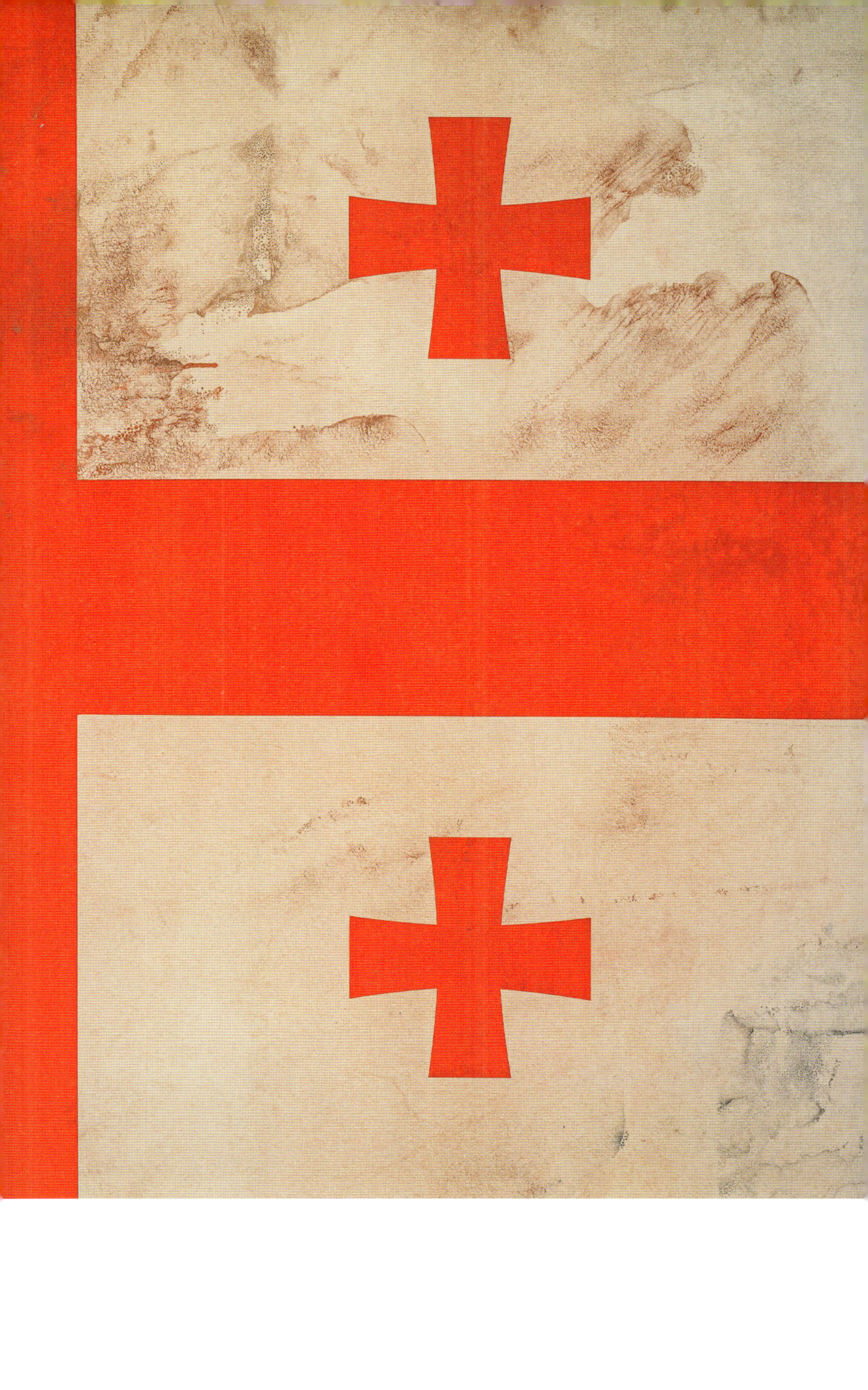

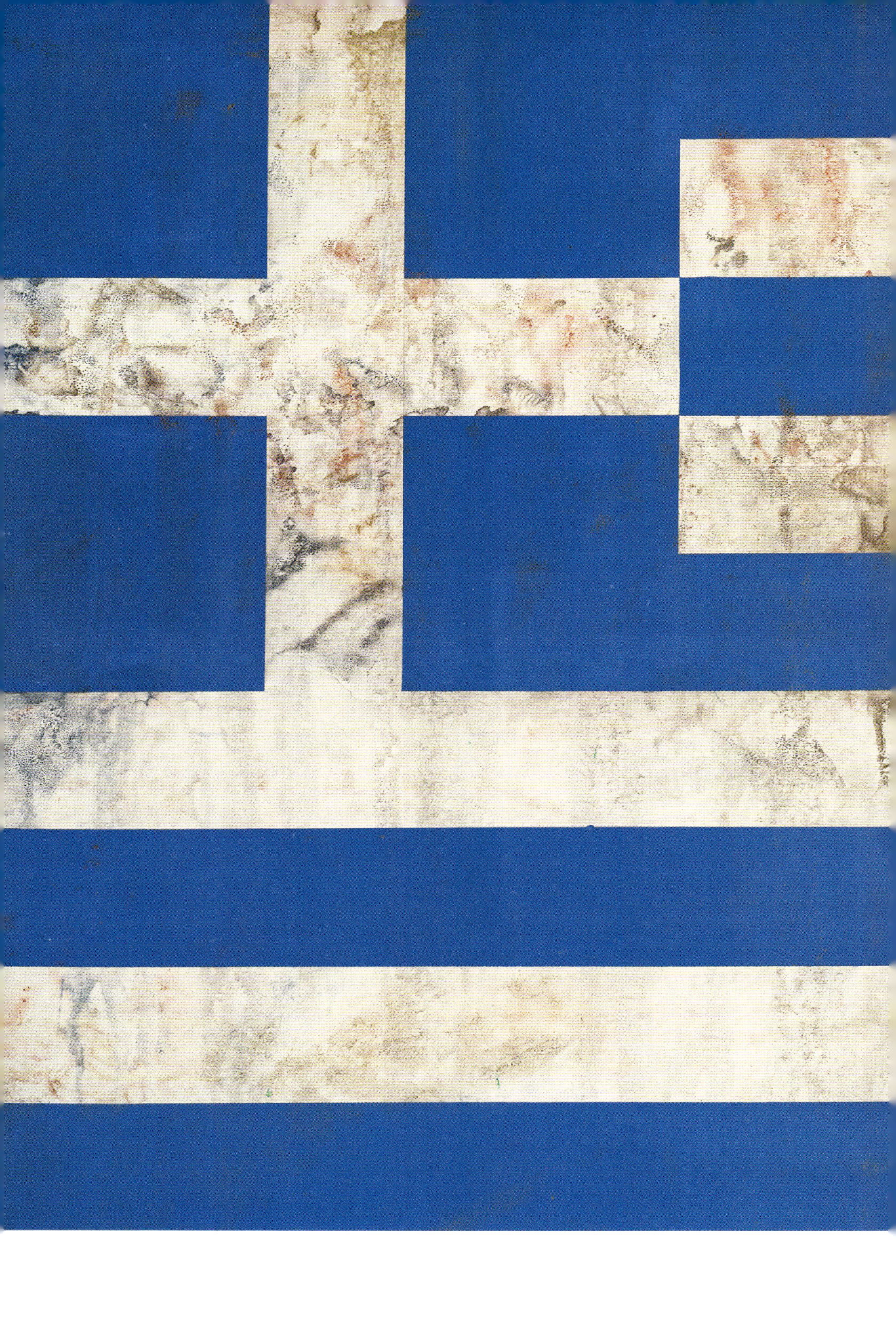

GREECE

P 36

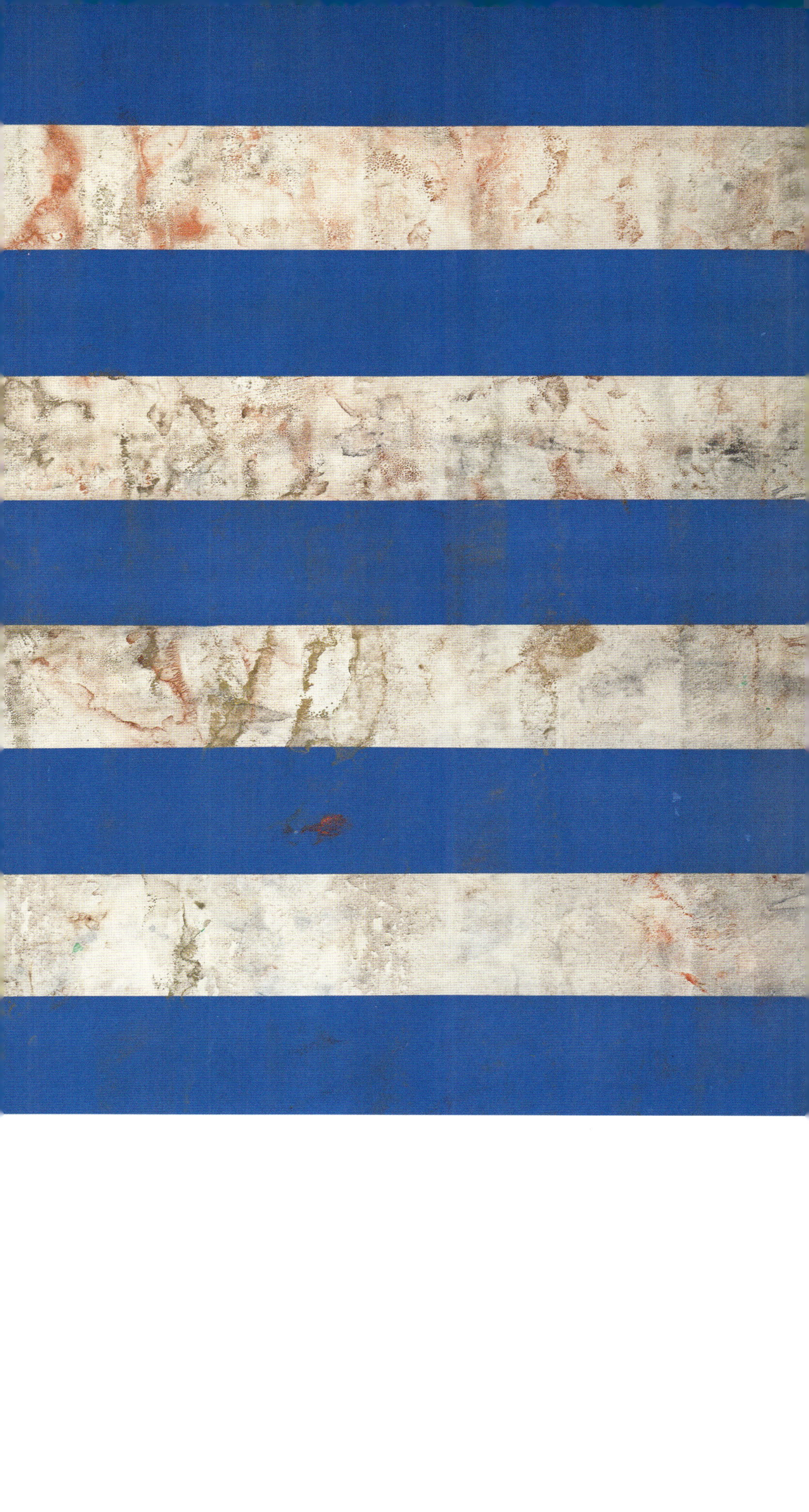

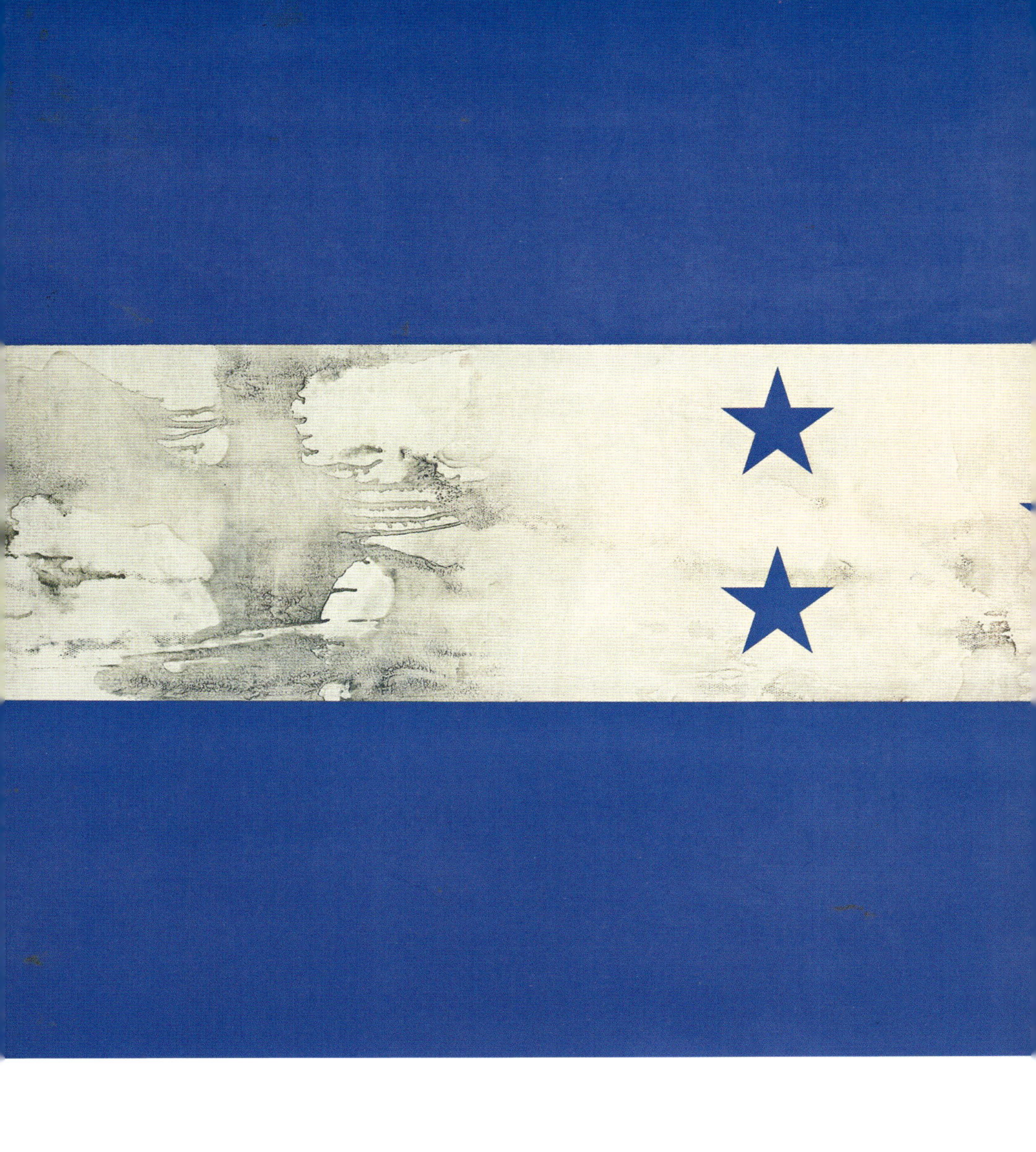

HONDURAS

P 38

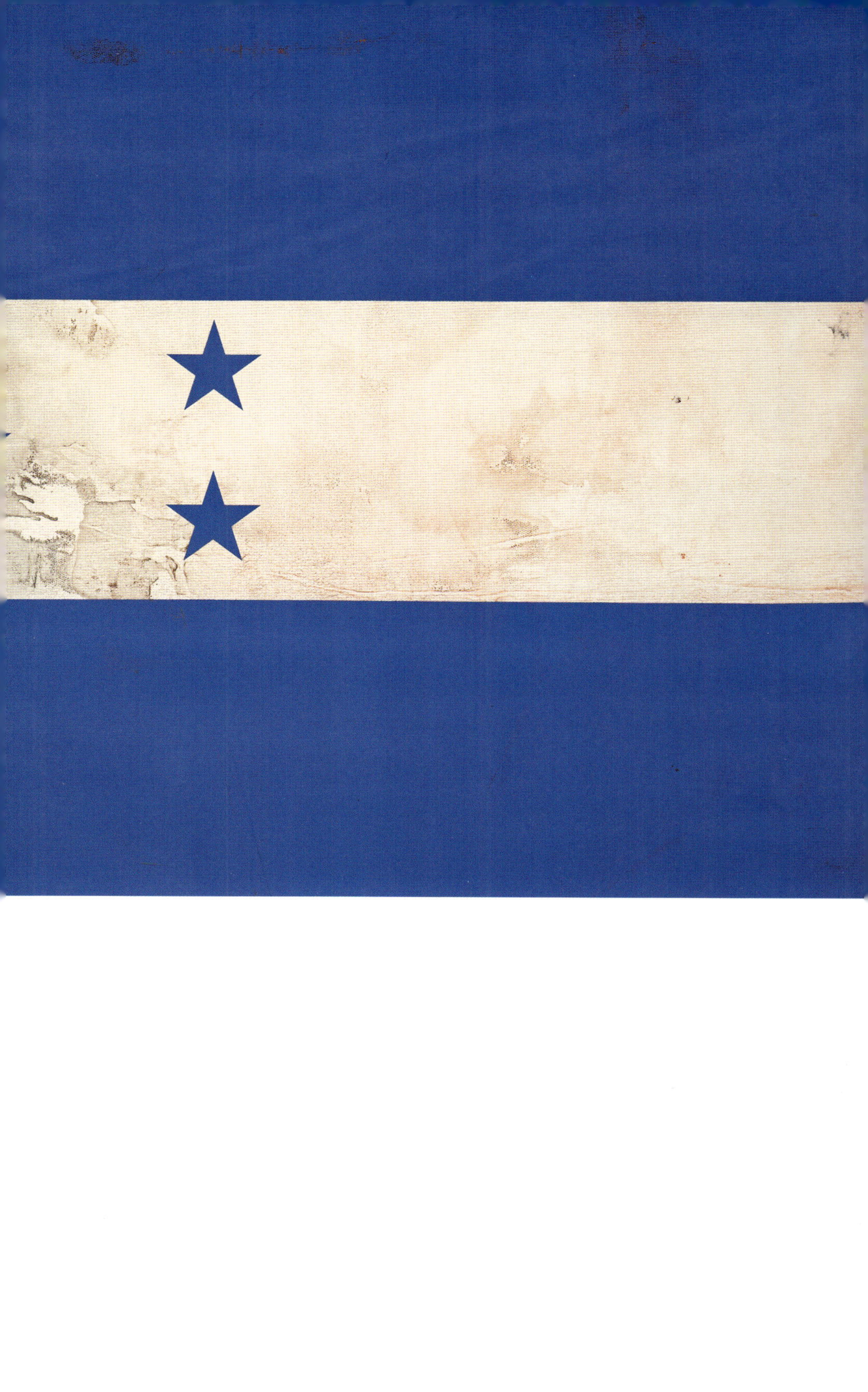

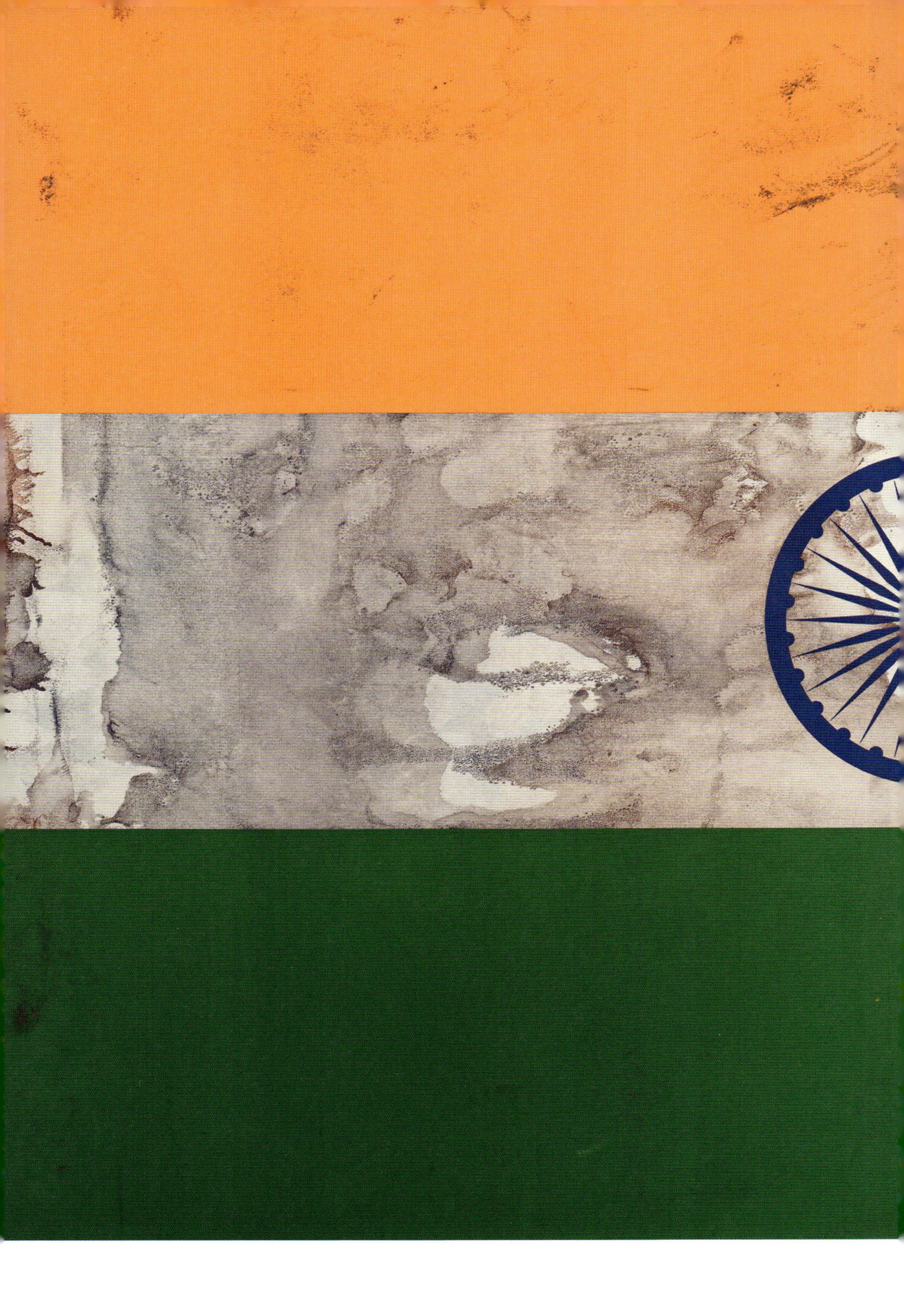

INDIA

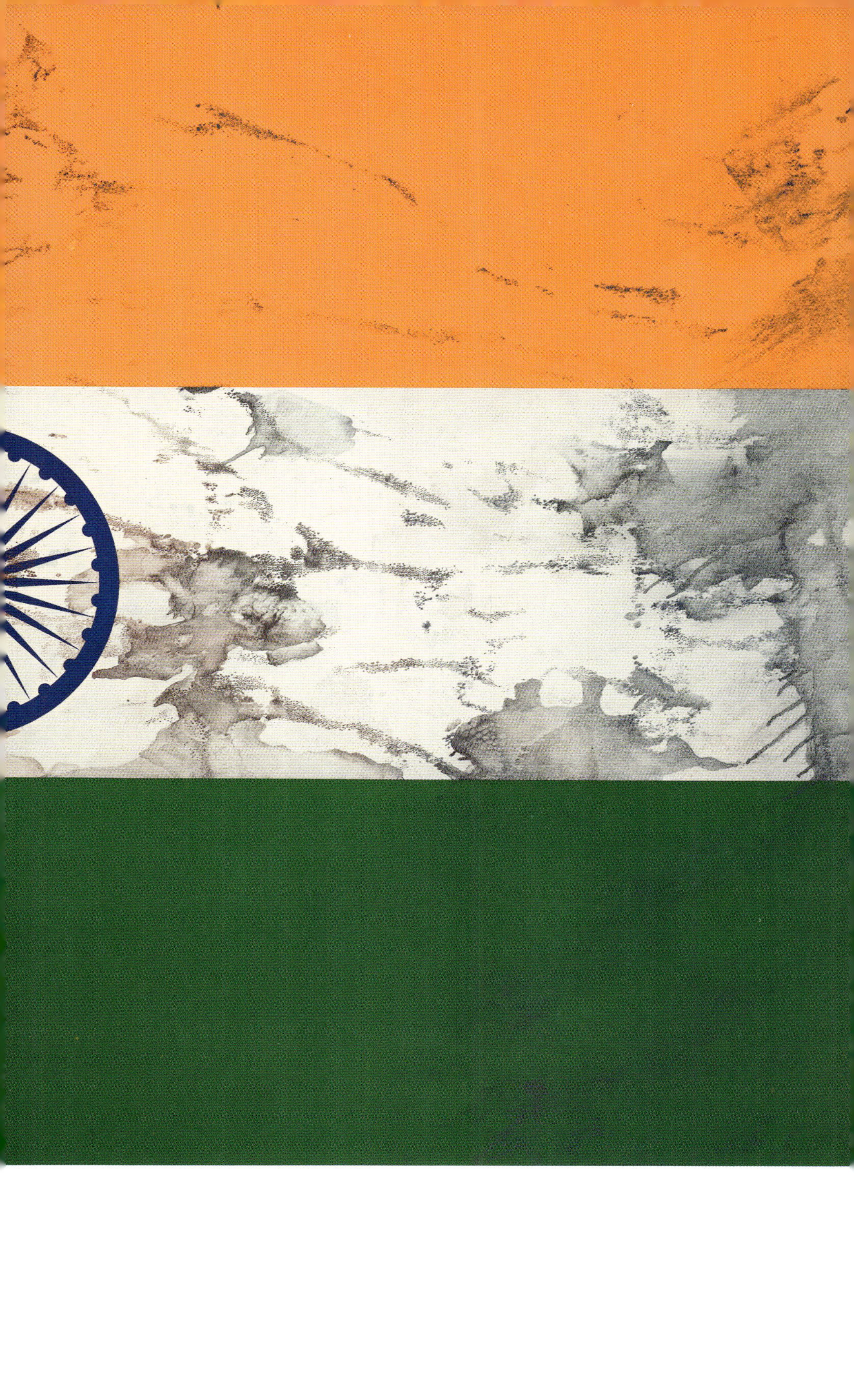

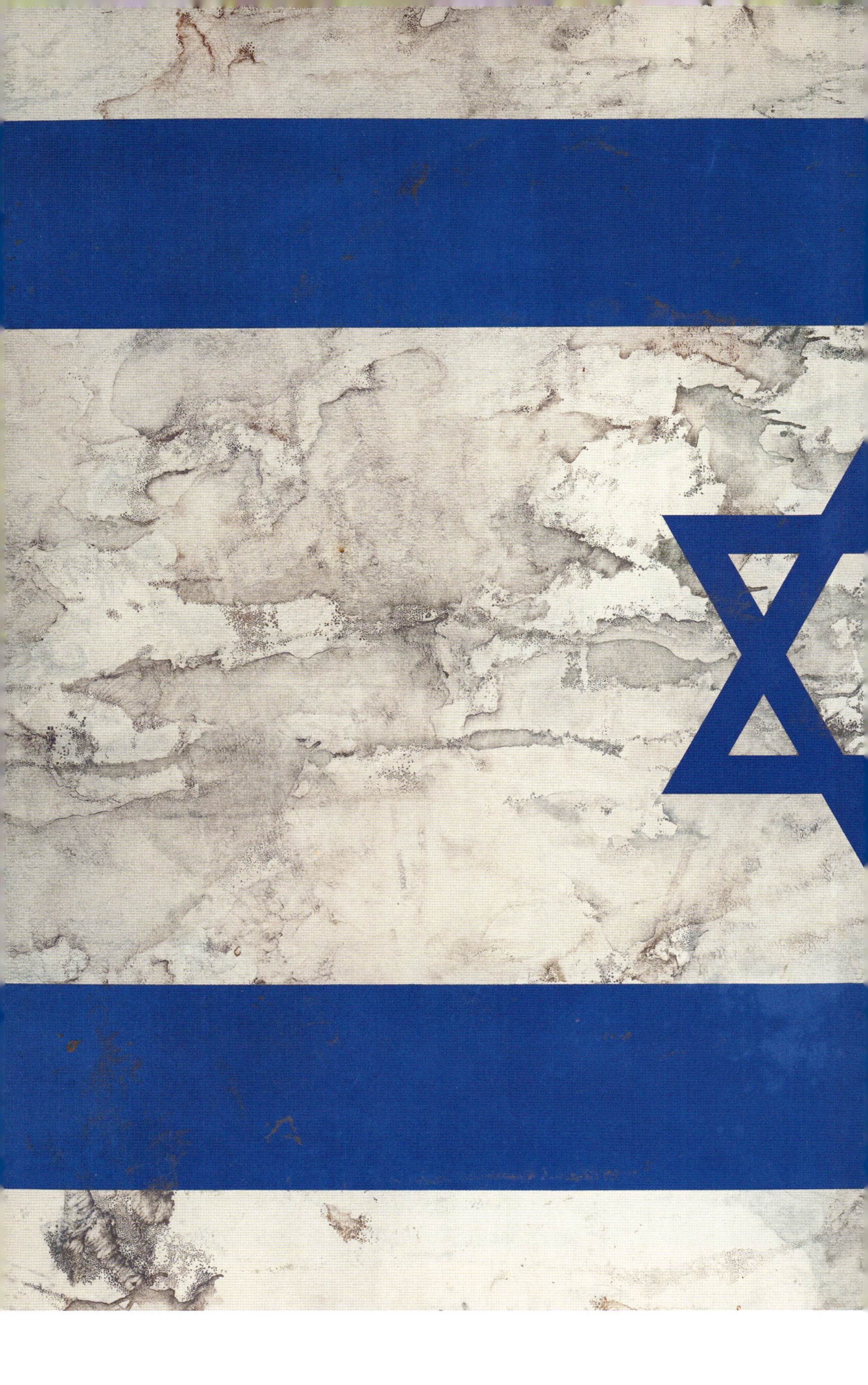

ISRAEL

P 42

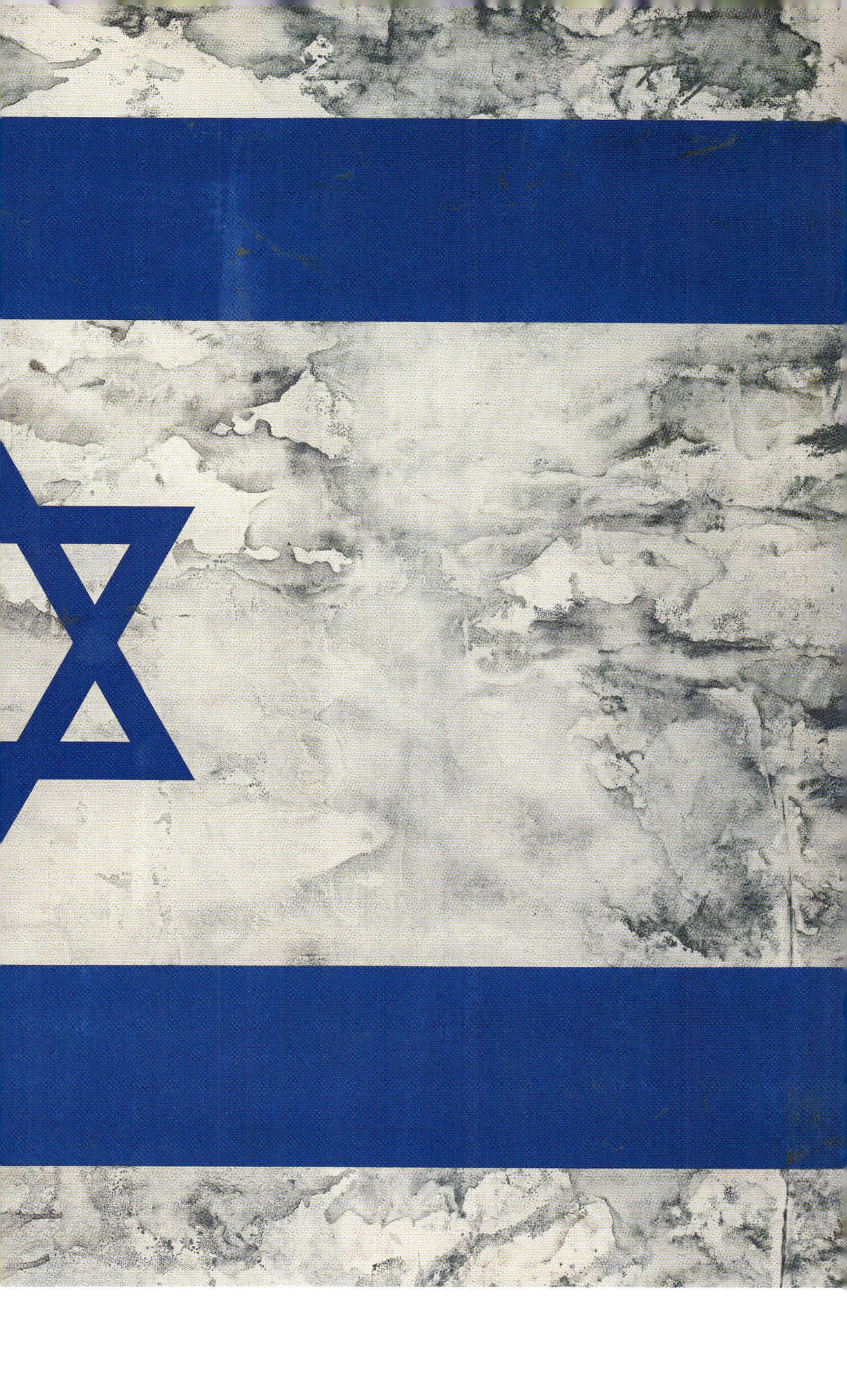

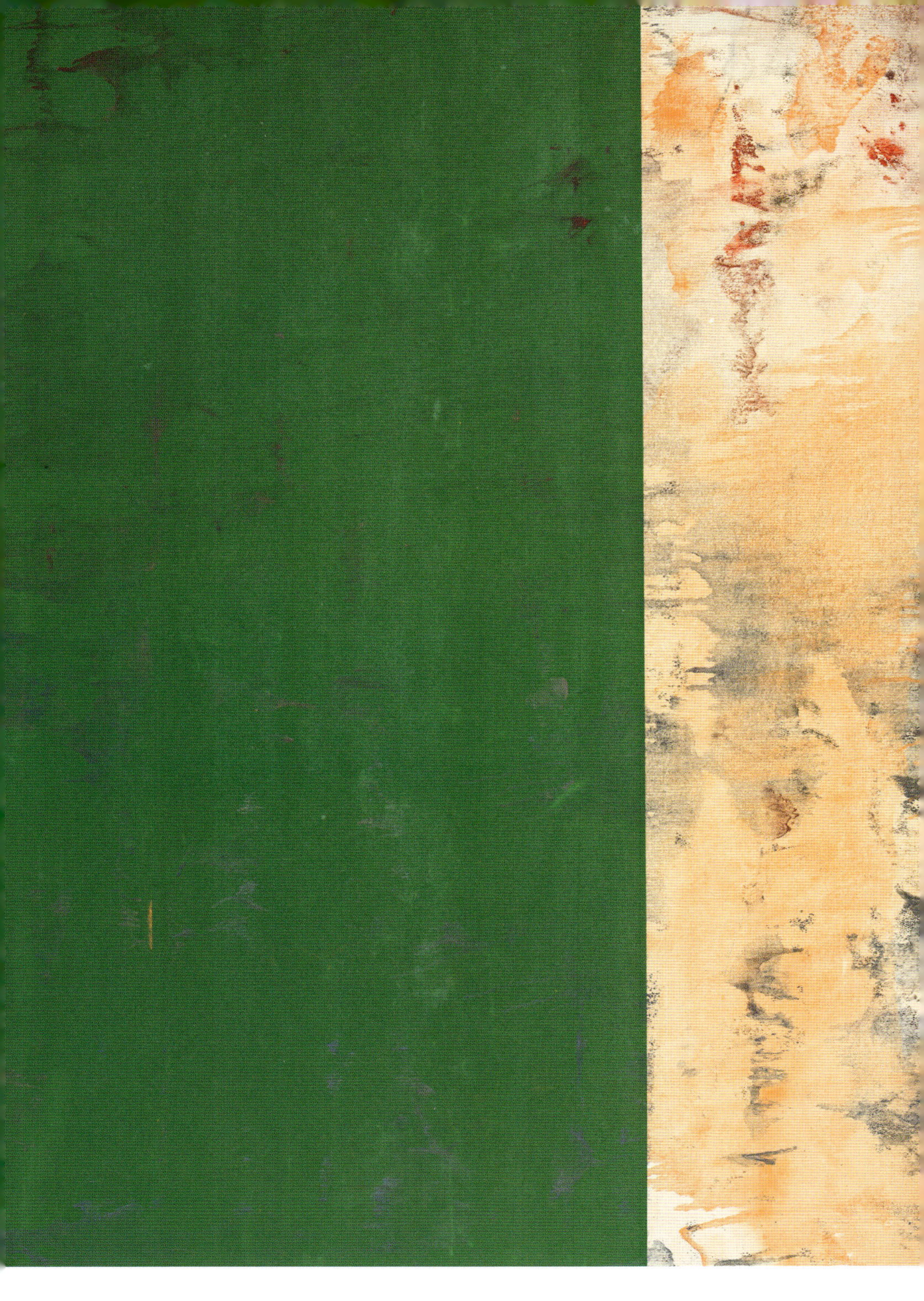

ITALY

P 44

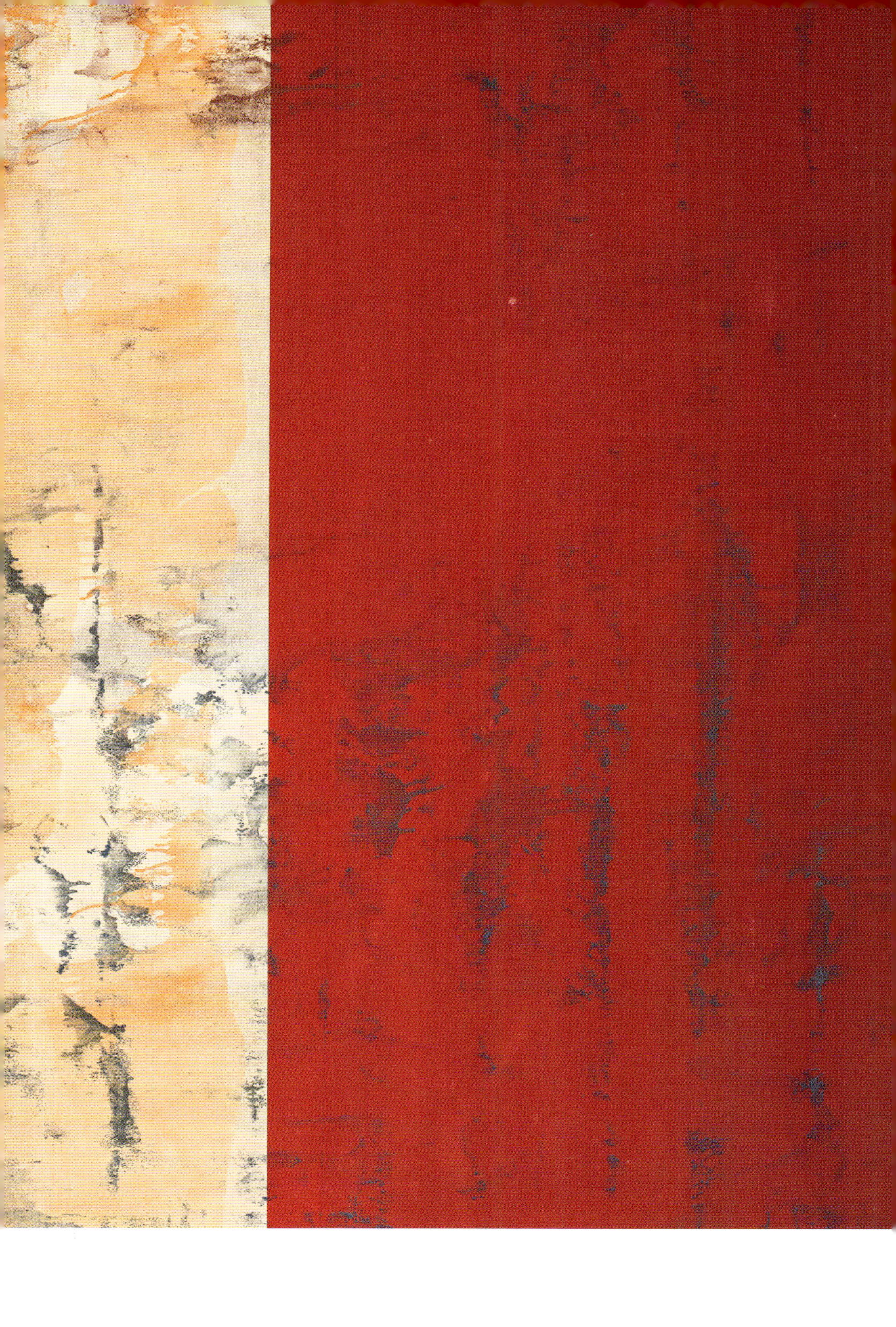

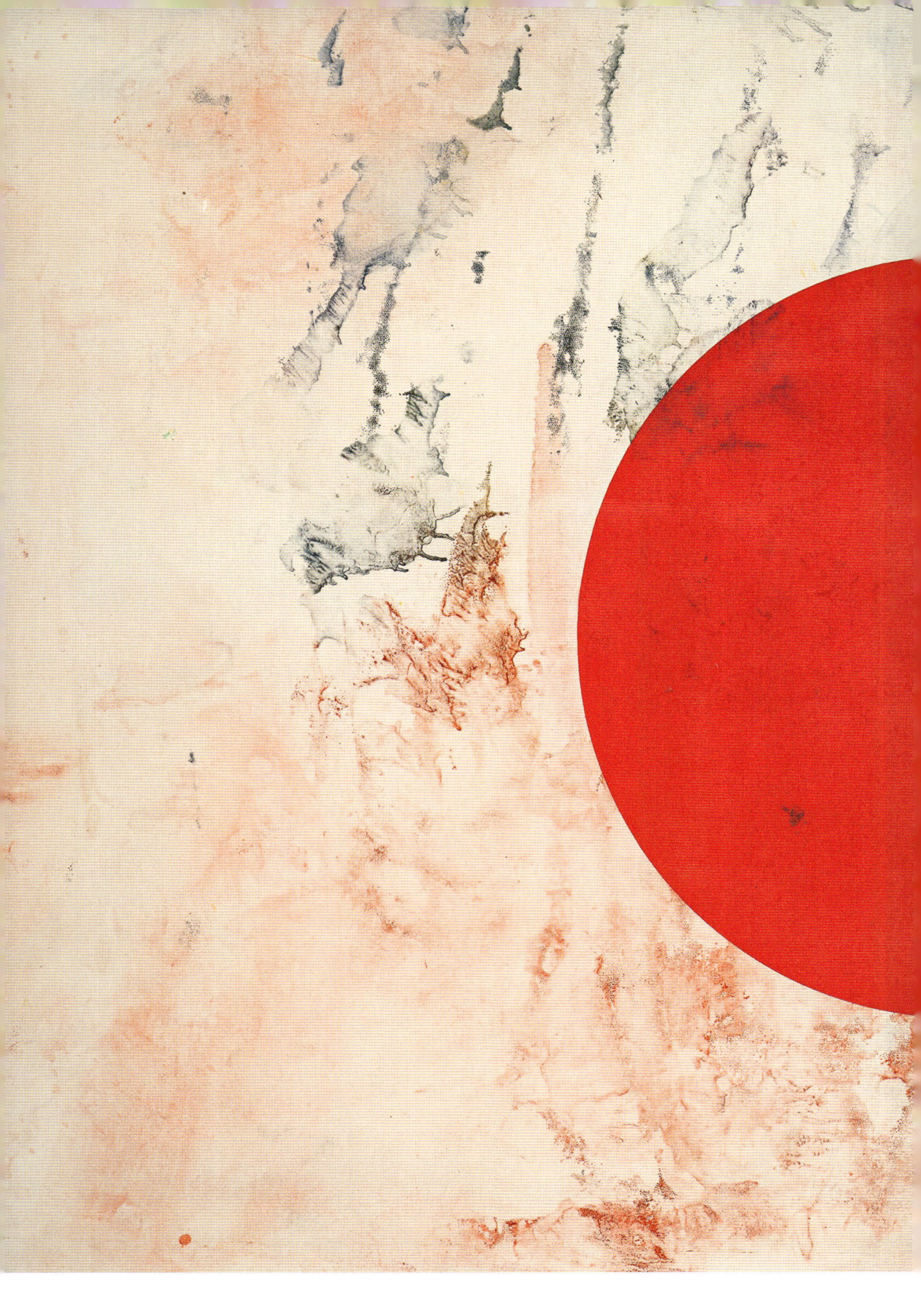

JAPAN

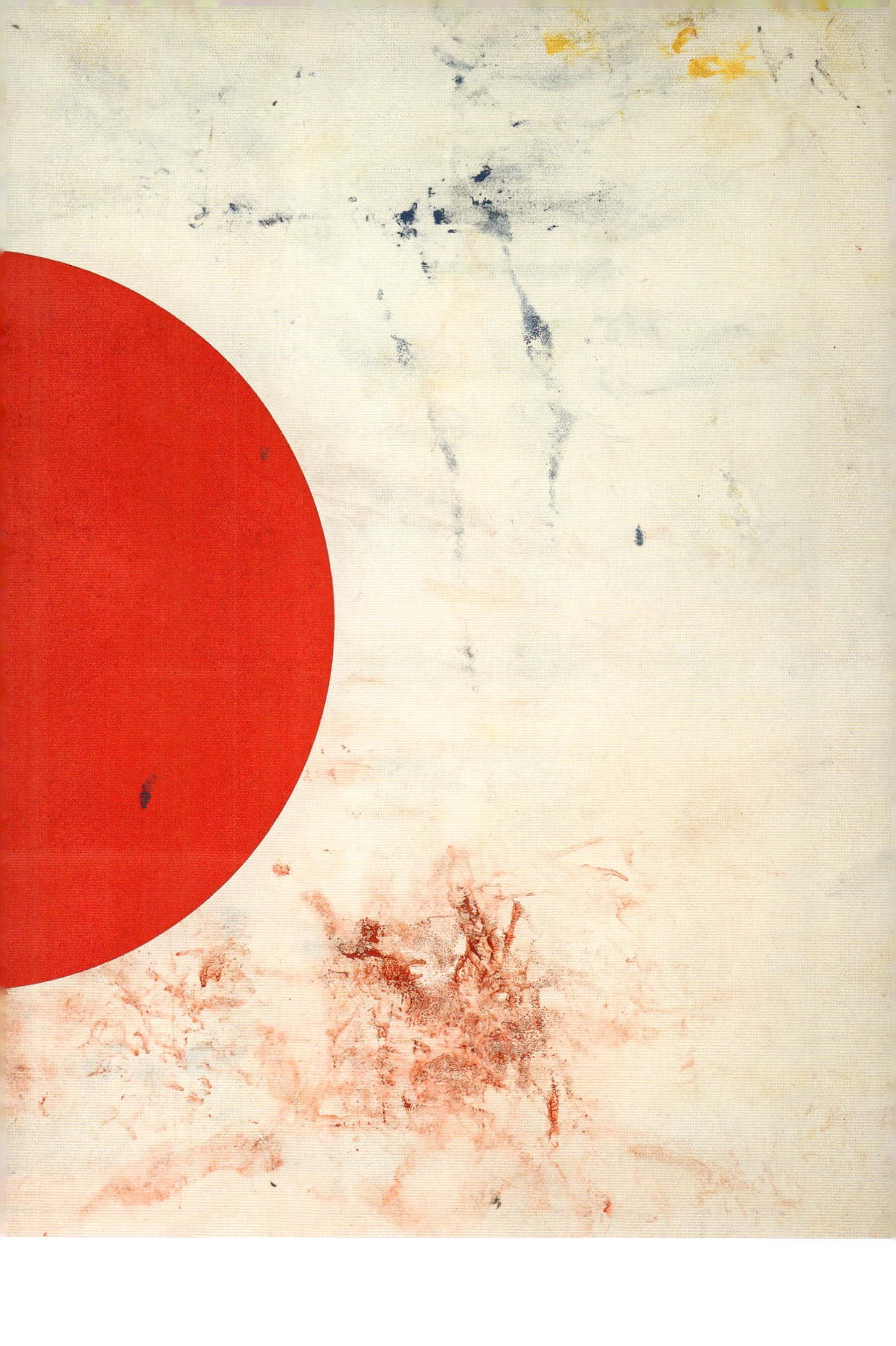

VEXILLATIONS
Dieter Roelstraete

I

What better day to embark on this writing journey than June 14, which I only to day discover is celebrated as Flag Day in my adopted home of the United State of America? It shouldn't come as much of a shock that such a day exists her at all. (You would be surprised, however, to learn how many countries aroun the world actually celebrate flag days of their own.) Though for one such as my self, raised on a steady and quintessentially Belgian diet of rabid anti-patric tism, America's fanatical, feverish attachment to its star-spangled banner ca be befuddling and bemusing at best, and alternately exasperating and infur ating most other times. In fact, seeing the US flag—so impossible to ignore, s bloody *omnipresent*, waving from every other doorpost or rearview mirror, grin ning at me from every other printable surface—can quite easily send me int paroxysms of utter rage.

Speak of a red rag to a bull: I am even annoyed, in a way, to see it show u in Fredrik Værslev's studio as a *painting*, one among many comparable pain ings "of" flags. (Is the fact that his most famous painting is of the Stars an Stripes one reason why I never really cared much for Jasper Johns?) This irra tional ire, I should note, far predates the revolting spectacle of Donald Trump— still US president at the time of this writing, alas—hugging and kissing the fla during one of his countless rallies. Flag Day, tellingly enough, is also the man' *birthday*—reason enough, if you ask me, to want to burn every single blood specimen in sight.

My sentiment may have its roots in the atavistic anti-Americanism of m youth, growing up as I did in a politically progressive microclimate in Wester Europe in the early 1980s in the shadow of Reagan's cruise missiles. Going t an antinuclear rally in Brussels in 1981 is pretty much my oldest political mem ory—a foundational and formative experience. It must have been around tha time, long before the onset of globalization, that I first started wondering wh the US flag in particular should be so absurdly ubiquitous, adorning T-shirts sneakers, sweaters, jackets, and jeans, and why any non-American would war to be caught dead wearing said emblem of what I already then, aged nine, intu itively understood to symbolize capitalist-driven imperialism at its most ma levolent. Reader, you can tell: I am clearly expertly placed to write about the a of the flag with levelheaded, detached neutrality, engaging in it as I do in th long shadow of "current events," which (who knows?) may no longer be all tha current by the time this text appears in print.

I am jotting all of this down at a time—the early days of summer 2020— of unprecedented civic unrest roiling US public life. The total number of fata ities claimed by the COVID-19 pandemic in the United States, a human-mad disaster if ever there was one, currently clocks in at around 125,000, and a across the nation, cities have seen mass-scale marches, looting, and the atter dant military-style police brutality in response to the state-sanctioned killing c a black man named George Floyd in the supposedly liberal bulwark of Minneap olis. And the Stars and Stripes, of all inanimate objects, once again proves to b the most dependable flash point of them all. *That fucking flag*. The ignominy c seeing it painted, *turned into art!*

Here is what New Orleans Saints star quarterback Drew Brees—not know for his progressive politics, so, not much of a surprise here—had to say abou the protests, quite a bit of which predictably involved a fair bit of flag burning, o June 3, midway through the most tumultuous week in the States in more than decade:

> I will never agree with anybody disrespecting the flag of the United States of America or our country. Let me just tell what I see or what I feel when the national anthem is played and when I look at the flag of the United States. I envision my two grandfathers, who fought for this country during World War II, one in the Army and one in the Marine Corp. Both risking

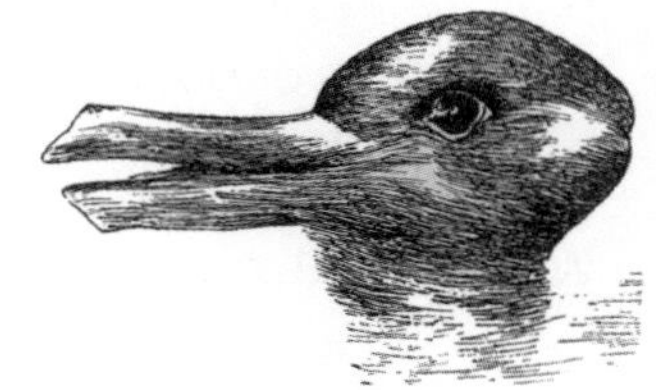

their lives to protect our country and to try to make our country and this world a better place. So every time I stand with my hand over my heart looking at that flag and singing the national anthem, that's what I think about.

This was evidently not well received by Brees's many African American teammates and sporting peers, the public faces of so much Black Life That Matters, leading him to contritely walk back some of his comments in the following days, concluding with a tweet addressed directly at Donald Trump, of all people, in these times of unparalleled racial strife and ever-tensing culture wars—wars fought out over symbols (flags, hymns, *face masks*, statues) more than anything else: "We must stop talking about the flag and shift our attention to the real issues of systemic racial injustice, economic oppression, police brutality, and judicial & prison reform. We are at a critical juncture in our nation's history. If not now, then when?" Let us be done with the flag waving and saluting. Let us be done with the noxious hyperbole of "symbolic capitalism"!

II

The US flag may be the most widely desecrated national symbol in postwar history. Predictably so, perhaps, given its unceasing worldwide visibility as both a wearable commodity and an icon of the culture of commodification. (One could dedicate an entire exhibition to the desecration of the US flag as an aesthetic operation—an exhibition made up entirely of desecrated flags, of Stars and Stripes *after* Jasper Johns.)[1] Still, it is somewhat surprising to learn that, the political passions aroused by this symbol notwithstanding, it is actually *not* illegal to desecrate or deface said flag. (It is in many countries around the world and Denmark holds the curious distinction of being the only country that prohibits the desecration of any flag *except its own*; how utterly Nordic.) As the American Civil Liberties Union, which has organized efforts against legislative attempts to ban flag desecration (including recently proposed constitutional amendments in 2004, 2006, and 2011), puts it:

> Our democracy is strong because we tolerate all peaceful forms of expression, no matter how uncomfortable they make us feel or how much we disagree. The US Supreme Court has affirmed and reaffirmed that the right to desecrate the flag is included in the Constitution's protection of speech. Flag burning and desecration is offensive precisely *because* it is political. Experience shows that the way to fight political expression with which one disagrees is not to outlaw it, as Congress has repeatedly sought to do, but to express disapproval.[2]

The irrational depth of the passions aroused by the flag may help us better understand the fabric of US society as essentially *theocratic* in its warp and weft. Its national ensign is easily compared, in this regard, to the flag of the Kingdom of Saudi Arabia, which features the Islamic creed or *shahada* as its central motif: "There is no god but Allah; Muhammad is the Messenger of Allah." Because of the obvious sanctity of the *shahada* Saudi Arabia guards its flag code with the utmost rigor: even the slightest violation of said code amounts to both desecration *and* the mortal sin of blasphemy. Understandably for a country that chooses to print the motto "In God We Trust" on its currency—another ubiquitous item that is regularly subject to the legal challenge of desecration—the fervor with which it venerates the flag is exposed as fundamentally *religious* in nature in the occasional occurrence of its *defacement*. Indeed, as the Australian-born anthropologist Michael Taussig has observed in his study on the subject:

> When the human body, a nation's flag, money, or a public statue is *defaced*, a strange surplus of negative energy is likely to be aroused from within the defaced thing itself. It is now in a state of desecration, *the closest many of us are going to get to the sacred in this modern world*.... Defacement works on objects the way jokes work on language, bringing out inherent magic nowhere more so than when these objects have become routinized and social, like money or the nation's flag in secular societies where God has long been put in his place. Defacement of such social things brings a very angry god out of hiding....
> Around me there is no sacrifice, nor much passion about sacred things. The disenchantment of the world still seems to me a largely accomplished fact. What exists now is perhaps best thought of as a new amalgam of enchantment and disenchantment, the sacred existing in muted but powerful forms, especially—and this is my central preoccupation—in its "negative" form as desecration. Then the almighty speaks—indeed, bellows.... No matter how crude, defacement and sacrilege thrive on bringing dead and apparently insignificant matter to life—as in the case, for instance, of the desecration of statues or money.[3]

1 Such an exhibition, which I do not recommend anyone set out to curate, would center on three major flag pieces by black artists: Dread Scott's *What Is the Proper Way to Display a US Flag?* (1988), David Hammons's *African-American Flag* (1990) 01 (more about this work shortly), and Pope.L's *Trinket* (2015) 02, that last undoubtedly the most powerful work made in this vein in the last couple of decades. Pope.L's mischievously titled *Trinket* debuted at Geffen Contemporary at MOCA in Los Angeles in early 2015: "a monumental, custom-made American flag (approximately 54 x 16 feet) hanging on a pole in the middle of the Geffen. During the museum's public hours, the flag [was] continuously blown by four large-scale industrial fans—the type used on Hollywood film sets to create wind or rain effects—and will be illuminated from below by a bank of custom theatrical lights. Over time the flag [appeared] to fray at its ends due to the constant whipping of the forced air, a potent metaphor for the rigors and complexities of democratic engagement and participation." See https://www.moca.org/exhibition/william-popel-trinket. A painting by Ed Ruscha from 2017 titled *Our Flag* bears a remarkable resemblance to Pope.L's *Trinket*. Jasper Johns's first *Flag*, now owned by the Museum of Modern Art in New York, dates back to the mid-1950s, and ninety more paintings based on the US flag followed in the years to come. Working a full decade before a tidal wave of youthful disenchantment and dissent engulfed the world (much of it sparked by sightings of the flag in question in one far-flung corner of the globe too many), Johns was in many ways the last artist who could afford to treat the star-spangled banner as a primarily (or even exclusively) painterly occasion ("things the mind already knows," in Johns's phrase). It is an irrecoverable naiveté that echoes knowingly in Værslev's irony-laden return to the subject.

2 "Flag Burning or Desecration," ACLU.org, https://www.aclu.org/issues/free-speech/rights-protesters/flag-burning-or-desecration. The issue of the transgressive charge of burning the flag in particular is complicated by the fact that federal law designates burning as the preferred means of disposing of the flag "when it is in such condition that it is no longer a fitting emblem for display."

3 Michael Taussig, *Defacement: Public Secrecy and the Labor of the Negative* (Stanford, CA: Stanford University Press, 1991), 1–3, 13, 43, my italics. Does Taussig's compelling hypothesis explain the visceral pitch of my feelings of irritation when encountering the US flag, as recounted in the opening paragraph? Maybe so. Taussig makes much of defacement's etymological root in the notion of *faciality*: "I take the face to be the figure of *appearance*, the appearance of appearance, the figure of figuration"—the *symbol of symbolization*—"the ur-appearance, if you will, of secrecy itself as the primordial act of presencing. For the face itself is a contingency, at the magical crossroads of mask and window to the soul, one of the better-kept public secrets essential to everyday life." Taussig, *Defacement*, 3. I am interested here in the pictorial asymmetry of face and flag: as an iconographic rule that could just as well be called a law, flags do not feature faces, and only relatively rarely living things. They are also never truly "faced" or come face-to-face with, ideally flying high above our heads. There is an obvious (if minor) element of defacement at play in rendering a flag as a painting, to be encountered at eye level, face to face, in a gallery of all places. Recent weeks of popular unrest across the United States may have seen some isolated instances of flag burning, but these have been dwarfed by the great reckoning that has befallen statuary, from Christopher Columbus to Philadelphia mayor Frank Rizzo. The toppling, removal, and occasional destruction of monuments and statues around the country is further proof of our era's paralyzing preoccupation with patrolling and policing the symbolic order, at the obvious expense of what one could call "real-world" issues and challenges (for instance Drew Brees's message to Donald Trump quoted above). On the other hand, it is precisely this disproportionate emotional investment in the realm of symbols that makes art matter more—indeed, that might potentially *make art great again*.

01

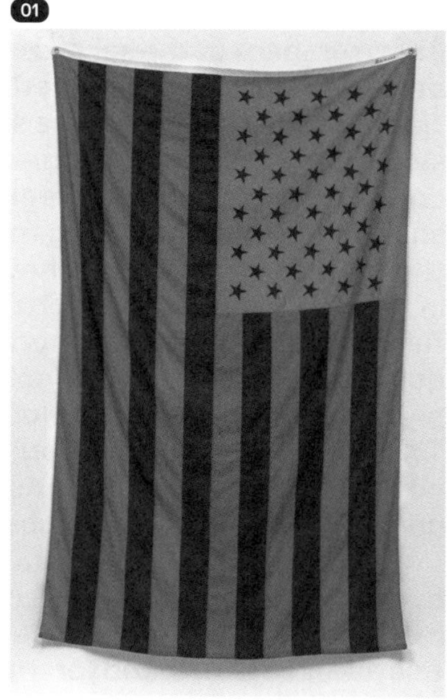

02

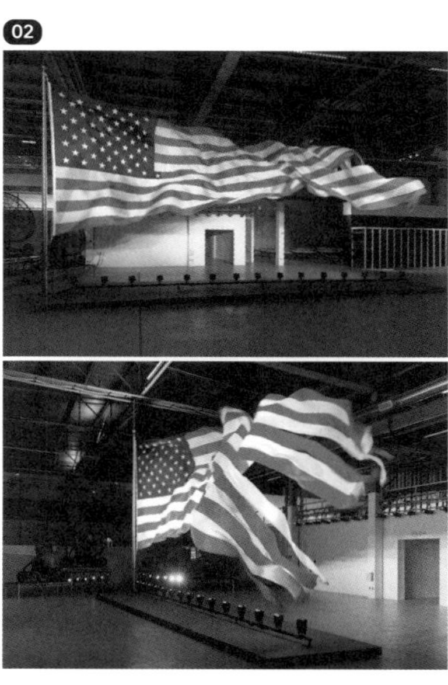

I bring in Taussig's discussion of defacement and desecration as the sole mobilizing remnant of the sacred in our otherwise bloodlessly secular lives in an ironi attempt to frame the rendering of flags as paintings or works of art—Værslev's "labor of the negative"—as somehow defamatory in nature. Looking at his version of the Stars and Stripes up close, for instance—in itself a strangely discomforting gesture that reeks of profanation[4]—I am inevitably drawn to th smears of red paint soiling the pristine right half of the painting. Predictably, i these apocalyptic times, they conjure the specter of all the violence committe in this flag's name, so much of it visited upon its own citizenry, the more forcefully and viciously so the more darker its citizens' skins. An old Jean-Luc Godar quip comes to mind: "It's not blood, it's red," to which the symbolists inevitably reply: "It's not red, it's blood!" The same symbolists who would likely exclaim "It's not a painting, it's a flag!" to which the formalists would object in turn: "It's not a flag, it's a painting!" Asked differently still, the question becomes: Is it a duck, or a rabbit? Is it a—*duckrabbit*? (There is no such thing—or is there?)

The reference here, of course, is to the duck-rabbit illusion made famou by Ludwig Wittgenstein in his *Philosophical Investigations*, published posthumously in 1953, a drawing I use as this essay's epigraph. Wittgenstein deploy this rebus as shorthand for the difference, among other things, between "seeing and "seeing as"—a distinction that evidently echoes in the perceptual challeng of Værslev's flag paintings, suggesting that we are always in some way forced t see either a flag *or* a painting, but never both at the same time. And so far, *I* hav mostly seen the flags. It requires a peculiar effort of will to see "just" the paintin and nothing else. It's something to do with the physical proximity to the *object* a hand—see my note regarding the reek of profanation—and the disappearanc of the *symbol* in the process of approaching it.[5]

There are clear echoes in Værslev's US flag of David Hammons's variou body prints from that other great period of flag burning, the late 1960s an early 1970s. Think, for instance, of *America the Beautiful* (1968), *Boy with Fla* (1968), *Pray for America* (1969), *Black First America Second* (1970), *Injustice Cas* (1970), and *Feed Folks* (1974), all of which paved the way for one of the august African American artist's best-known and most iconic pieces, *African-America Flag* (1990), "a clever amalgamation of the stars and stripes with Marcus Garvey's nationalist palette of red, black, and green—a new insignia (with all of it latent irony) for an African American nation."[6] Hammons is a major point of reference in Værslev's world, and the ghost of the former's tarp paintings eeril hovers over much that the latter artist has undertaken in recent years, mos notably his *Canopy*, *Sail*, and *Window Paintings* (2012–18).[7] The more powerfully felt transgression in Værslev's star-spangled banner, however, is (fittingl enough) of a much more crudely economic kind, implied in the simple fact that once shown inside the gallery alongside a dozen other flag paintings just like it the Stars and Stripes can be yours to own for the same amount of money tha it would cost to acquire the painted flags of, say, the Central African Republic Djibouti, Niger, Somalia, or—speaking of cosmic retribution—other "shithol countries" like it.[8]

4 I am taking recourse to the olfactory metaphor here in continued reference to Taussig's spiel on the defacement-faciality dialectic: "Defacement evokes a prehistory of the face as sacrifice, as does Georges Bataille where he rewrites Darwin and Freud with their histories of the almighty consequences of man's ascent to the upright posture from the crouching ape. *This* is the long sought-for source of repression, Freud crowed to his muse in Berlin, Wilhelm Fliess, because the sense of smell, finely attuned to the anus and genitals of the Other, thereby lost its ascendancy over the senses once man strode forth on two legs. Henceforth the eyes were regnant." Taussig, *Defacement*, 4. The flag, with its inherent insistence on distancing through elevation, is but one powerfully abstracted symbol of this reign of the visual, optic, ocular. Flags fly their finest at the safe remove of the submissive eye's arm's length (see note 3 for more on the defacement-lite dynamic of Værslev's flag paintings). It is worth noting, finally, that the aforementioned olfactory simile is no mere metaphor, thanks to the artist's liberal use of turpentine in producing these works' literal essence.

5 Anne Wagner found a solution of sorts for this problem in the following reading of Jasper Johns's *Flag* as an emblem of a quintessentially *national* idea of art, of (modern) painting as an arch-American form—a reading conducted, we should add here, in the shadow of the 2006 midterm elections, occurring in an almost unrecognizably different United States: "What matters is not whether it is a flag or a painting, but why the two—the symbol and the practice—have been so intimately married, till death do them part." Anne Wagner, "According to What: Jasper Johns's *Flag*," *Artforum*, November 2006, https://www.artforum.com/print/200609/according-to-what-jasper-johns-s-flag-11920.

6 Apsara DiQuinzio, "David Hammons: Printing the Political, Black Body," Wattis.org, n.d., https://wattis.org/view?id=382. Hammons's *African-American Flag* has gone on to lead a life very much its own. I included it under another name, *U.N.I.A. Flag*, in a 2015 exhibition I co-curated with my former colleague Naomi Beckwith at the MCA Chicago titled *The Freedom Principle: Experiments in Art and Music, 1965 to Now*, and it reappeared most recently in battered, bruised, and tattered guise under the title *Oh say can you see* (2017), a work that I have only seen show up in print once, namely as an accompaniment to the lengthy Hammons feature by Calvin Tomkins, "David Hammons Follows His Own Rules," *New Yorker*, December 2019, https://www.newyorker.com/magazine/2019/12/09/david-hammons-follows-his-own-rules.

7 It would lead us too far afield to exhaustively address the mirroring of Hammons's uses of black plastic garbage bags, torn industrial tarps, and worn-out blankets and towels in Værslev's appropriation of canopies and sails, but it is worth noting in passing how Hammons's crypto-modernist ciphers of homelessness and urban decay—often deployed to cover what look like large exercises in gestural, lyrical abstraction—contrast with Værslev's melancholy markers of leisure and shelter (or leisure *as* shelter). An interesting precedent for Hammons's tarp paintings can be found in turn in the work of Sam Gilliam, a lone African American proponent of the color field painting school whose monumental sagging canvases shed an interesting light on Værslev's painterly pedigree.

8 "On January 11, 2018, during an Oval Office talk with several US senators about protecting immigrants from Haiti, El Salvador, and African countries in a new immigration package, President Donald Trump unleashed a word that Americans aren't accustomed to hearing from their president. 'Why are we having all these people from shithole countries come here?' Trump reportedly asked. (He later denied having said this.)" Ibram X. Kendi, "The Day *Shithole* Entered the Presidential Lexicon," *The Atlantic*, January 13, 2019, https://www.theatlantic.com/politics/archive/2019/01/shithole-countries/580054/.

III

Back in 2008, I was peripherally involved in the staging of the fifth Berlin Bien
nale, curated by Adam Szymczyk and Elena Filipovic, titled *When Things Cas*
No Shadow. One of the invited artists was Daniel Knorr, a Romanian-born resi
dent of Berlin whom I would subsequently collaborate with and write about on
number of occasions. Knorr's installation was simply titled *Nationalgalerie* (Na
tional Gallery), and consisted of a suite of fifty-eight flags, each measuring 36
by 280 centimeters, strung up, garland-like, along the square roof of Ludwi
Mies van der Rohe's iconic Neue Nationalgalerie in Tiergarten, one of the bien
nial's primary venues. Most of Knorr's flags consisted of standard-issue vertica
bands of color (no heraldry, no symbols), which enhanced the work's crisply min
imalist, hard-edge aesthetic—a formal reading facilitated by the fact that non
of these banners corresponded to any existing countries, nations, or territo
ries. Indeed, this being the so-called national gallery, erected in the war-scarre
heart of the country that took nationalism to its most destructive, genocida
extreme, a passerby casting a furtive glance would have assumed a deadpa
allusion to the pageantry of nationhood in the fictionalized abstract. Only a su
premely knowledgeable viewer, a vexillologist (more about this word soon) o
truly encyclopedic inclinations, would have been able to divine the proper sourc
es invoked in this coolly festive, gnomic display: they represented fifty-eigh
German student fraternities culled from the wide swath of German history,
history in which such associations have famously functioned, more often tha
not, as incubators for the aforementioned strain of rabid nationalism. None o
this intel impressed another Berlin-based artist acquaintance of mine, howev
er, who upon seeing Knorr's signature piece flutter in the summer breeze de
livered the following crushing four-word verdict: "I hate flag art." That pointe
poignant observation has stayed with me ever since, and in some way or othe
continues to haunt my every encounter with flag art, most of which *I like*, courte
sy of my own long-standing personal interest in heraldry and symbology. Includ
ing that of Værslev today.

It is easy to figure the source of this affront. Flags, even those of some
thing as arcane and remote as a nineteenth-century student association, con
note nations and national identities, and few identifying mechanisms kno
how to rile the denizens of the global art world quite like these markers of te
ritorial belonging, of earthly anchorage and plain *groundedness*. This is a
the more keenly felt in a city like Berlin, where the vast majority of art-makin
and art-appreciating individuals are actually foreign nationals, forever on th
move and go. So many rootless cosmopolitans make this city their temporar
home that a respectable number of them were grouped, some ten years ago, i
a survey show titled *Based in Berlin*—not, tellingly, truly *living* in Berlin. A show
case of this nature could also have been named, more accurately even, "Fly
ing In and Out of Berlin." Flying in and out of its EasyJet hub in Schönefeld, to b
more precise.

It does help that even though Berlin too has a flag of its own—and is there
fore not entirely exempt from the tyranny of territorial symbolization—its en
sign, at least, sports the disarming likeness of a bear. Animals have a way o
deflating the grandiose claims of any flag. Furthermore, and much more impor
tantly, there is the massively fraught matter of the politics of flag hoisting an
flag waving in Germany at large. It is often suggested that only with the comin
of the FIFA World Cup to Germany in 2006 did it become popularly acceptabl
again to fly the Schwarz-Rot-Gold from private windows, cars, and balconies
Interestingly enough, the largest flag painting I know of was made by Gerhar
Richter in the late 1990s for the lobby of the then newly opened Reichstag i
Berlin, depicting that very same *Schwarz, Rot,* and *Gold* and measuring a vertig
inous twenty-one by three meters."[9] Whereas class and sexual identity in pa
ticular continue to power the political engine of art-world topicality, the *bêt*
noire of national identity has long been shrouded in taboo—as implied in th

9 These are all minor milestones in the recent history of the ideas of nationhood and nationalism—the history Værslev's painting project partakes in—which in the mere twenty years that I have been writing professionally about art and culture have been through a roller-coaster of twisting fates. The return of nationalist fervor we have witnessed in the political turn toward right-wing populism across the globe since 2016 would have been hard to imagine back in the year 2008 of said Berlin Biennale—a year capped off with the election to the US presidency of a young African American man named Barack Hussein Obama.

suggestion that to ask anyone "where they're from" is considered something o a microaggression these days.

The contemporary art boom of the last quarter century is a quintessen tially global phenomenon, inextricably tied up with a borderless economy but tressed by cheap international air travel, mobile communications technolog the gospel of 24/7 connectivity, and the rise of the Airbnb paradigm—a world view in which nationality is deemed irrelevant at best, and a source of embar rassment and stigma at worst.[10] (If forced to choose at all, artists generall prefer to "belong" to cities rather than countries—a curious throwback to th medieval ethos of fiercely localized guild life, perhaps, the heraldic complemen of which can be found in today's FC Barcelona or Bayern München jerseys: sym bols of local belonging it is OK to sport, even if only ironically.) The national flag as a symbol of bounds and roots, of an almost metaphysical *immobility*, direct ly contradicts everything that makes art contemporary: mobility and flexibility rootlessness and *freedom*.[11]

⚐10 It is no exaggeration to claim that in the current condition of worldwide, COVID-19-enforced lockdown and the subsequent reinforcement of national borders and sovereignties, contemporary art as a sociopolitical phenomenon has quite simply been forced into a quasi-vegetative state. The art world that I know and grew up in has ceased to exist for now. All of which makes the sheer act of painting national flags appear so painfully, poignantly timely—a sense that must certainly have occupied the artist's mind while painting "his" Norwegian flag in particular. When were artists last (or, indeed, ever) forbidden to cross borders? When were we last forced to stay "home" like we are right now, quite literally grounded? As a matter of fact, I had planned to fly to Oslo from Chicago in April 2020 for the sole purpose of seeing Værslev's paintings up close before embarking on this writing project. Who wants to write about paintings without seeing the damn things in person? The exponential spread of the novel coronavirus has forced the entire world into quarantine mode, the longest stretch of immobilization I have ever endured in my professional life. Nations, and national borders, have regained much of their political reality of late—an especially painful realization for a visa-carrying European exile in *this* America. The very idea of the national flag means something radically different today than it did a mere half year ago, and the very act of painting national flags today has likewise taken on a radically different meaning, urging a reconsideration of what may constitute a properly national—as opposed to generically post-national—art.
⚐11 "We no longer have roots, we have aerials," in McKenzie Wark's felicitous phrasing. See her *Virtual Geography: Living with Global Media Events* (Bloomington: Indiana University Press, 1994), X. Which begs the question: Could there exist such a thing, then, as a flag representing the *United States of Art*? There already exists an unofficial hymn for this speculative body's leftist wing, after all. It is called the "Internationale," the music for which I was proud to learn was composed back in 1888 by a Belgian socialist called Pierre De Geyter. On a related note, one compelling example of flag art of a quasi-historical vintage can be found in Felix Gmelin's *Farbtest, Die Rote Fahne II* (Color Test, the Red Flag II, 2002), a two-channel video work coupling Gerdt Conrad's tracking shot of students running through the streets of late-1960s West Berlin waving a red banner with the artist's own (decidedly more subdued) restaging of the original 1968 event more than thirty years later. The red flag of our long-lost Marxist utopia is the one banner it is still (relatively) safe, I dare say, to hoist in art's post-national circles. Let me put it this way: Yevgeny Khaldei's *Raising a Flag over the Reichstag* 03 is a better picture than Joe Rosenthal's *Raising the Flag on Iwo Jima* 04, and they were taken a mere two and a half months apart in the spring of 1945.

03

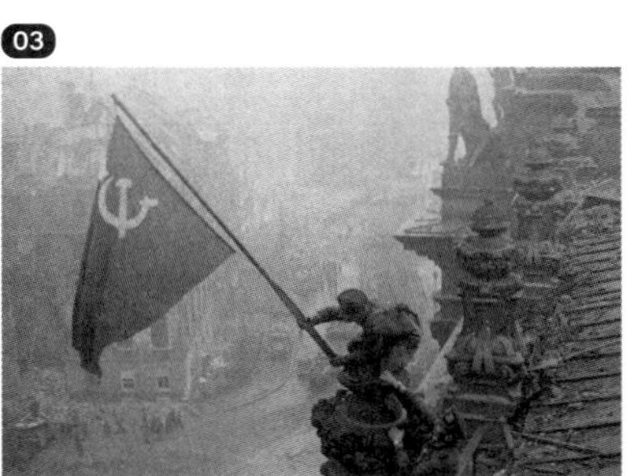

04

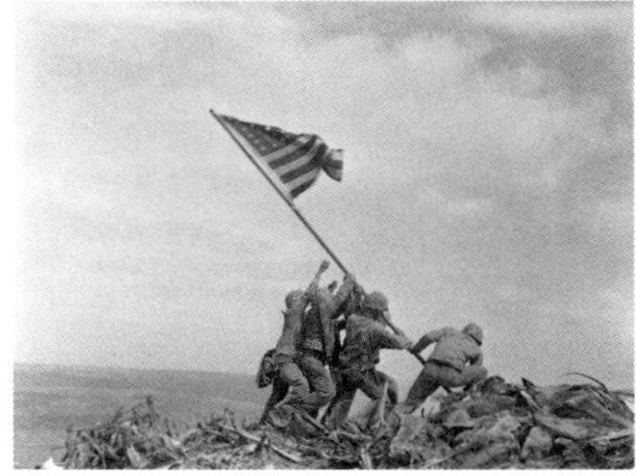

IV

In an email exchange predating our current homebound predicament, Værsle
noted that “this project . . . has been in the making in one way or the other sinc
the summer of 2006, when I was first confronted with the minimalist, hard
edge flags of the Swedish artist Olle Bærtling hanging outside the Moderna Mu
seet in Stockholm.” 05 (To which he added, crucially: “I am not interested i
Bærtling’s ‘free’ minimalist language, merely the potential of the flag as a pain
ing,” signaling the clear continuity of these flag paintings with the canopy, pal
let, and sailing works that I wrote about at length on another occasion, and t
which we will have occasion to return at a later stage.)[12] I was admittedly onl
dimly aware of Bærtling’s work beforehand, and wholly ignorant of said flags
but, Bærtling’s predilection for emphatic asymmetries and diagonals notwith
standing, it is easy to see the formal parallels with Knorr’s *Nationalgalerie* an
a host of other artists who have explored the pictorial and/or sculptural poten
tial of this airborne, and quintessentially *public*, platform. Other artists whos
work comes to mind here are Daniel Buren, Christo, Jeremy Deller, Mike Kelley
and Matt Mullican. Somewhat predictably, perhaps, women artists do not ap
pear to feel especially drawn to the form, with the noteworthy exception of Ma
ilyn Minter’s *Resist Flag*, unveiled on Flag Day back in 2017, as well as the olde
example, of particular importance to Værslev’s personal development as an ar
ist, of Cady Noland’s iconic *Oozewald* 06 from 1989, depicting the alleged as
sassin Lee Harvey Oswald at the moment of his own violent death, his painfull
contorted mouth stuffed with a rolled-up US flag.

Flags are minimalist ur-forms, possibly the oldest extant examples of mir
imalist art in the broadest sense, and certainly the single most economical spe
cies of “monument.”[13] Such a marvel of minimalist design as the Japanes
flag, for instance, dates back centuries. The official adoption of the so-calle
Sun Disc in February 1870 was the culmination of hundreds of years of abstrac
tion and reduction. The French *tricolore*, the global symbol for the struggl
to achieve *liberté*, *égalité*, and *fraternité*, was taken into official use in Febru
ary 1794. The revolutionary appeal of its spartan design is nowhere more palpa
ble than in Eugène Delacroix’s *La Liberté guidant le peuple* (Liberty Leading th
People) from 1830, the first major painting to feature a national flag in all its bol
monochromy. The Finnish flag, officially adopted in February 1920, is said to ow
its arresting combination of snow white and lake blue to the nineteenth-centur
nationalist bard Zachris Topelius. Tonga’s curious riff on the blood-soaked cru
ciform austerity of Switzerland’s national ensign (itself dating back to the Mic
dle Ages) was first flown in 1875. Who even knew that Tonga had been a countr
for that long? And last but certainly not least comes the minimalist masterpiec
that is the Austrian flag, dating back to the early years of the thirteenth cen
tury, with one legend concerning its origin citing the crusader Battle of Ptole
mais (part of the Siege of Acre) in 1191 as its source.[14]

Finally, closer to the actual flowering of the minimalist aesthetic in moc
ern art in the late 1950s and 1960s, consider the bold visual language of Africa’
newly emancipated former colonies, conjuring memories of contemporane
ous works by the likes of Josef Albers, Ellsworth Kelly, Barnett Newman, Kennet
Noland, or Frank Stella (or Olle Bærtling, for that matter)—to wit, the flags ac
opted by Madagascar in 1958, Niger in 1959, Nigeria in 1960, and Botswana i
1966. (Recommended listening: Robert Hood’s minimalist techno masterpiec
Minimal Nation from 1994.) The crucial tension here is clearly between the un
versalist, proto-globalist claims of minimalism’s visual language and the seem
ingly parochial business of nation building, leading us to wonder, inevitably, hov
parochial the idea of a universalist claim might be (or how parochial the ide
of nationhood as such). Is the minimalist creed in image making an exclusive
ly Western affliction, comparable to the ideological biases embodied in the U
and French flags? Is the Japanese flag a global icon, an appropriately “Eastern
image, or just another “Western” picture after all?

⚐12 Dieter Roelstraete, "Version," in *Fredrik Vaerslev as I Imagine Him*, ed. Gunnar B. Kvaran (Zurich: JRP Ringier; Oslo: Astrup Fearnley Museet, 2018).

⚐13 Which brings us back to the quintessentially *public* nature, in conception and origin, of the vexilloid form, so dependent on airflow and wind to make its rousing presence felt—an aspect plainly denied in Værslev's *paintings* of flags, destined as they are to lead a motionless, flattened existence on walls inside interior, quite likely *private* spaces. This is yet more proof of the magical workings of desecration, complete with the morbid overtones of iconoclasm as a revolt against an animistic view of the object world. The notion of the flag's animistic charge—the mystery of its status as a not-so-inanimate object—returns us to Michael Taussig's earlier observations on defacement and sacrality.

⚐14 Here is one leading vexillologist's version of its genesis: "Duke Leopold V was supposedly granted these arms by King Henry VI, based on the battle-bloodied tunic of the duke, which had remained white only where covered by his wide belt. Losing his standard during the fray, Leopold supposedly raised his tunic as a rallying point, and the design was subsequently made official." Whitney Smith, *Flags through the Ages and across the World* (New York: McGraw-Hill, 1975), 47.

05

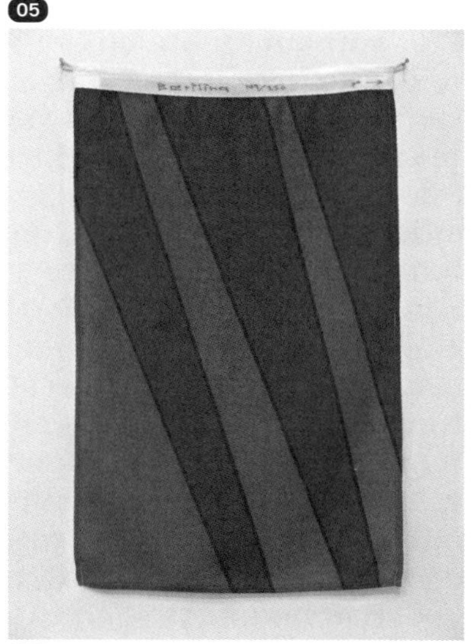

06

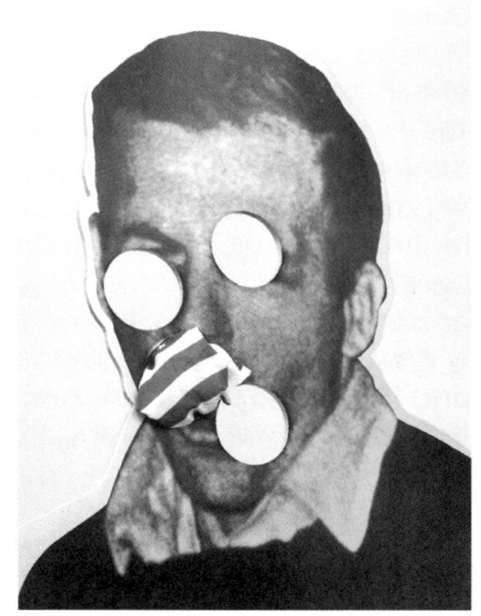

The study of the history, symbolism, and usage of flags is known as vexillology, after the Latin word for flag, *vexillum*. Vexillography, correspondingly, is the technical term for the art of flag design. (The title of this text is an allusion to that of a famous piano piece by the French composer Erik Satie, "Vexations," which consists of a single short theme that, according to Satie, must be played 840 times in succession, such that a performance of "Vexations" can last anywhere from fourteen to twenty-eight hours. I like the titular suggestion of displeasure and irritation in this lullaby-like composition, reminding me here of the vexing nature of the flag's appearance in art—the "problem" of flag art.) Both terms owe their coining to the late Whitney Smith, the founder of vexillology as a discipline of academic merit. As an active vexillographer, Smith also designed the national flag of Guyana, which was taken into official use on May 26, 1966, and which also appears, as a painting, in Værslev's *World Paintings*.

Smith is the author of various books on the subject, the most comprehensive of which is *Flags through the Ages and across the World*, first published in 1975—the source of much that I have learned about the phenomenon in question. Introducing the history of the form, Smith avers:

> Flags are a universal characteristic of human civilization. With the exception of the most primitive societies and of nomadic peoples, it appears that every culture has invented for itself flags of one kind or another—with a remarkable similarity of form observable throughout the world.... So strong is the tradition of flags, we may not be far from the truth in surmising that there is a law—not of nature, but of human society—which impels man to make and use flags. There is perhaps no more striking demonstration of this than the fact that, despite the absence of any international regulation or treaty requiring the adoption of a national flag, without exception every country has adopted at least one.[15]

I am interested in two claims here, made in the book's opening chapter. One is the (evidently debatable) suggestion that flags are a hallmark of sedentary life—that "planting" a flag may have been part of the same agricultural revolution that, millennia ago, decisively steered human history away from the culture of nomadism and toward the social contract of the settlement (see our earlier discussion of the contemporary nomad's fear of flags). The other is the ambiguous notion of the flag as a *standard*, as a powerful tool in the global arsenal of *standardization*, a cornerstone, in turn, of the international infrastructure built out in the nineteenth century—the golden age of nationhood.[16] The formal concept of the standard in particular, related to that of the blueprint or template—familiar forms for Værslev, a former graffiti artist whose preferred mode of painting continues to involve the spray can—helps us better understand Værslev's vexillographic interests from a purely painterly perspective. Painting flags is an exercise in relinquishing much of the decision making involved in art's implicit injunction to always start from scratch, to "make it news." Here, the words of Jasper Johns obviously do ring true 07. These are "things the mind already knows"—one could expand and paraphrase, calling flags things the *hand* already knows—impervious, that is, to the romantic vagaries of invention. There is no room here for any originality in the painting act as such, and very little opportunity for letting loose the illusion of mark making, for the mirage of gesture as the sacramental proof of authorship. (Flags cannot be amended or improved upon.) It is worth reiterating here how Værslev's obsessive use of the aforementioned spray cans, along with masking tape, further helps to ensure the very meaningful physical distance between the canvas and the artist's "signature" touch.[17] Moreover, the painter of flags can be certain of one thing for sure: his or her paintings will be universally legible. It is an aspiration of truly utopian intent.[18]

15 Smith, *Flags through the Ages and across the World*, 32.

16 The key text here is Keller Easterling's seminal *Extrastatecraft: The Power of Infrastructure Space*, which unfortunately does not address the role of flag design in the international aesthetic of standardization, despite the flag's singular communicative, symbolic power as a pivotal "infrastructural" element. In a chapter devoted to the telecommunications revolution and its role in shaping the modern world—a process in which flags certainly played their part—Easterling notes that "for many historians, the first meeting of the International Telegraph Union in Paris in 1865 may be worthy of no more than an obscure technical footnote." However, "telecommunications historian Anton Huurdeman has noted that it was the first international agreement concerning most of Europe since the Peace of Westphalia in 1648." Regarding the entanglement of communication systems and nation building, Easterling goes on to remark: "When Armand Mattelart, a leftist sociologist and scholar of communication media, writes that 'Communication serves first of all to make *war*'"—consider the obvious historical roots of flag usage in military operations—"he refers to the Chappe graphic telegraph that Napoleon used almost exclusively for military purposes." An amusing footnote continues: "The only civilian use [of the Chappe telegraph] was to broadcast the results of the lottery." Keller Easterling, *Extrastatecraft: The Power of Infrastructure Space* (London: Verso, 2014), 135–40.

17 In a conversation with the author, Værslev claimed that he has not touched a paintbrush in eight years. Spray cans have been his imaging weapons of choice for close to a quarter century—long before he became an artist, indeed, a *painter*. It is likewise important to note that he paints on the floor, further increasing the distance from the ever-threatening curse of the "artist's hand." An epic ream of deliberate, finely strategized efforts thus goes into producing an impression of a certain effortlessness—of the absence, that is, of authorial mark making.

18 In the artist's insistence on the utopian possibility of this universal legibility—of what could truly be called an art "for all"—there is an element in the art of flag painting that is curiously redolent of the (leftist) populist politics of Op art, whose practitioners likewise dreamed of an art intelligible to all, free from the classist mechanics of artistic or art historical literacy. It is worth keeping in mind the historical convergence of certain strands in the unjustly maligned Op art movement with the "hard edge" aesthetic of artists like Albers, Bærtling, Noland et al. Who would deny the pure perceptual ("op") power of, say, the Japanese flag?

07

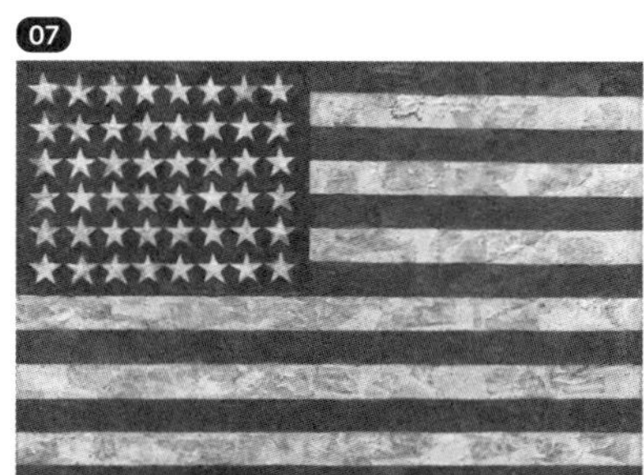

Smith locates the origins of modern flag design and usage in the heraldic arts known for the exact kind of aesthetic excesses that the proto-minimalist agenda, in all its globalizing reductive fervor, sought to weed out. Heraldry, in turn “had its origins in the practical need for recognition of soldiers on the battlefield, following development of helmets which covered the face.” However “after heraldry’s loss of practical relevance on the battlefield and the growth of new social classes whose power depended on wealth and royal favor as much as on military prowess”—surely the invention of firearms and other technological developments in the art of war likewise played a role in this process—“coat of arms began to suffer from an artistic degeneration evident in some of the exaggerated designs of the sixteenth century and later. Even before this, heraldry had become a plaything for the ruling classes. While one can appreciate the color and the drama of the tournament, its ostentatious theatrics had little relevance to practical affairs of state or warfare.”[19]

Speaking here of the moment when the late Middle Ages began to give way to the early stirrings of the modern spirit, Smith continues: “Development of symbols on land in Europe were paralleled by fundamental changes at sea Until roughly 1500 most vessels did not travel great distances. Naval flags consequently did not come into their own until the age of wind-powered craft, or roughly from the sixteenth century through the nineteenth. (Flag usage has decreased in the era of powered vessels, partly because of the speed at which the travel and partly because radio and other systems have altered radically the traditional visual identification of ships.)”[20] The aforementioned dynamic of standardization and aesthetic simplification, in other words, has *naval* roots, in the double use of *sails* as *flags*, and *flags* as *sails*. It is no coincidence that the modern era is so often said to have begun with the dawning of the age of oceanic exploration, ushering in the great Copernican uprooting of our times, increasing the importance of a truly global sign language, thus marking the beginning of our era of unrelenting sameness.

✳
Interlude (duck/rabbit; flag/painting):
“*You’re* a fucking inanimate object.”
Ralph Fiennes as Harry Waters in *In Bruges*, 2008
✳

⚐19 Smith, *Flags through the Ages and across the World*, 44.

⚐20 Smith, *Flags through the Ages and across the World*, 44. In an interesting aside expanding on said "ostentatious theatrics," Smith notes how "while changing tactics of warfare were making the use of heraldry of lesser importance on the battlefield, the tournament of the fifteenth century became the justification for the display of arms and banners. Here was an appreciation for the beauty and majesty of standards, pennants, trumpet banners, crests, tabards, horse trappings, and similar armorial displays *for their own sake*" (52). The italics are mine, pointing to the conception of said pageantry as a form of art, wholly in line with a medieval aesthetic sensibility that sought to find beauty in all of being. However, "the death of King Henry II of France in 1559 from wounds received in a tournament largely ended the popularity of this sport" (52). This surely makes for a rather unique origin story of early modernity—born from the demise of jousting.

VI

Fredrik Værslev has made paintings of the flags of Austria, Belarus, Cyprus, Denmark, England, Faroe Islands, Finland, France, Greece, Israel, Italy, Latvia, Monaco, Nauru, his very own Norway, Russia, Scotland, South Africa, South Korea, Switzerland, Taiwan, the United Kingdom, and, as mentioned, the United States. Although the future destination of these works does not directly concern us here, it is easy to imagine the appeal some of these paintings will hold for private collectors and/or collecting institutions "belonging" to said nations. (For a US collector to acquire the US flag, for instance, requires an interesting exercise in managing irony that enriches the work's straightforward painterly appeal. Right this very second, however, it seems like a hard sell. Værslev has also, "however," made paintings of Cambodia, Central African Republic, Djibouti, Egypt, Guyana, Honduras, India, Japan, Laos, Lebanon, Lesotho, Liberia, Niger, Nigeria, Panama, Saint Lucia, Seychelles, Somalia, Sudan, Timor-Leste and Tonga: "shithole countries" in the far-flung Pacific, East Asia or Latin America. The world, in other words, of "others." What is a white man like him—and a Norwegian at that, painting the flag of his motherland at a time when that, too, has long ceased to be a guilt-free pleasure[21]—doing, painting flags of African countries and showing them in galleries—*white cubes*—in Milan and New York right now? His is an especially contentious position to take in the current climate of heightened sensitivity to so-called cultural appropriation. Here, at long last, comes the first mention of *appropriation art*, when white writers everywhere are increasingly admonished to stick to "white" subject matter, and subject matter "of color" is increasingly cordoned off to privilege treatment by writers of color first and foremost. The intriguing insinuation that Værslev's flag paintings may figure in the broader historical context of appropriation art must be left unexplored here, but it is clear that in the case of his great example David Hammons, the notion of appropriation is evidently key, and that this notion also informs much of Værslev's earlier works, such as the canopy, sail, trolley, and window paintings. Unsurprisingly so, given appropriation art's centrality to the postmodern challenge to authenticity, authorship, and the politics of gesture.

Although it would be a stretch to read *World Paintings* as a sustained reflection on these perils of cultural appropriation—in the framework of which it is nonetheless fair to retort, for now, that *all* culture is appropriation, or that there would be no culture *without* appropriation—whiteness is without a doubt one of the project's core concerns, if only in the literal meaning of the potential of color, and the color of potential. What unites the flags of Austria, Belarus, Cyprus, Denmark, England, Faroe Islands, Finland, France, Greece, Israel, Italy, Latvia, Monaco, Nauru, his very own Norway, Russia, Scotland, South Africa, South Korea, Switzerland, Taiwan, the United Kingdom, and the United States with those of Cambodia, Central African Republic, Djibouti, Egypt, Guyana, Honduras, India, Japan, Laos, Lebanon, Lesotho, Liberia, Niger, Nigeria, Panama, Saint Lucia, Seychelles, Somalia, Sudan, Timor-Leste, and Tonga is the simple fact that they all have white in them. This is no mere (or not just a) symbolic rhetorical gesture, as white is considered the color of peace, in the world of vexillography and beyond, as well as the color of a certain *supremacy* in the world at large. It is a basic function, in the first instance, of Værslev's decision to paint on raw canvas—that is, "naturally" white cotton, allowing even the (seemingly) untreated bands of white in his flags to become an integral part of the painting, to simply appear *painted*, manufactured. This white signals the blank space of possibility—the very essence, if you will, of art. Its allegorical force is best appreciated in the soiling of the bands of white on the right-hand side of the US flag, an instance of conscious corruption and pollution already alluded to earlier on in this text. It is worth noting in this regard that Johns's iconic US flag from 1954 was followed a year later by his *White Flag*, its pride of place in the collection of the Metropolitan Museum in New York now obviously scarred by the controversial entanglement of whiteness and national belonging. It is the untreated nature of th

⚐21 In a conversation with the author,Værslev reflected on his childhood and youthful memories of the harmless pageantry surrounding the widely flown and wildly popular Norwegian flag, its international aura as a signifier of Nordic niceness and self-reliance strengthened in part by its popularity as a fashion accessory (it is the informal logo, among other things, of the Italian outerwear brand Napapijri). Here too, however, the extreme right's violent hijacking of nationalist agendas across the globe has irreversibly altered the emotional landscape of flag display. The Norwegian flag can never be the same again after the terrorist atrocities committed for its whiteness' sake by convicted mass murderer Anders Breivik in July 2011. Consider, also, that the Norwegian flag has made occasional appearances in Thor Steinar-designed apparel, the longtime garb of choice, of German manufacture, for neo-Nazis of all stripes. On a related note, and pointing back to Trump's infamous remark about Africa's "shithole countries" (see note 8): in that very same tirade, the US president whined that the United States should be encouraging more immigrants from "countries like Norway." To which Torbjørn Saetre, a politician representing Norway's Conservative Party in a municipality near Oslo, was among the first to respond (via Twitter, of course): "On behalf of Norway: Thanks, but no thanks." Ironically, at the time of this writing Norway has effectively shut its border to entrants from the United States.

white cotton substrate that, on a technical level, interests Værslev here, and s shrewdly syncs this body of work with earlier projects such as the canopy, ter razzo, trolley, and window paintings, all of which challenge the received idea o a painting's "finish," blurring (pun intended!) the boundaries between finishe and unfinished, painted and unpainted, and highlighting the tension, entirel central to the work of Fredrik Værslev as a whole, between the idea of mastery— the realization that one has "made" a great painting—and the general avoid ance of authorial mark making.[22] Nowhere is such mark making harder to avoi than when working in white.

In choosing to paint only flags that have white in them—those pristin stretches of nothingness that can (and *should*) never be kept "pure"—Værsle has built the lowly toil of erasure that is so fundamental to his practice (sub traction being as crucial to his working method as addition, turpentine as lib erally applied as paint) into the very fabric of these works' visual success. Fo what makes a flag painting like *Egypt* or *Syria* "great," in the final analysis— the painting, that is, that the artist is after—is this basic play of material con trasts between the blinding thickness and immaculate sheen of its perfectl constructed bands of black and red—the triumph of *color* at its most sanguin and opaque—and the sobering smirk of its lightly soiled, smeared white— the very picture, oh so satisfying, of *imperfection*.[23]

Returning, in conclusion, to the matter of whiteness as a symbol for "world peace (as well as surrender), a final word on these works' curious overarchin title (borrowed, as it so happens, from none other than Martin Kippenberge seems in order: *World Paintings*. Paintings "of" the world, then—think of ther as a species of realism, as well as landscape paintings in the sense alluded to i note 23. In the email exchange already referred to, Værslev pondered the vari ous semantic possibilities opened up by even the most basic of installing choic es. What does it mean for the US flag to be hung right next to the Russian fla (today, at least, during what feels like the twilight of the Trump presidency), c the Israeli flag next to its Egyptian counterpart, or Cyprus opposite Greece Such juxtapositions would likely reduce the paintings in question to their con tent alone, whereas the coupling of, say, the Danish and the English flag woul likely lead us down the dead end of pure, interchangeable form.

Furthermore, does a painting of a flag appear more flag-like when see among other paintings of flags, or is its Platonic flag-ness more likely to emerg in the splendid isolation of the single work of art? Conversely, does a dens grouping make us lose sight of their meaning (the question of its meaning be ing, among other things, whether a flag must always be a picture of domination and make them appear more purely painterly and pictorial? The commercia implication is clear: Should these paintings be sold as a group? Should they b kept together as a group? When deemed "better together," we may catch glimpse in them, perchance, of a more complete, harmonious world—of trul *united* nations. Can a politically abrasive or overly didactic hang seduce us wit the power of form alone? Again, one more time: Can we ever see *just the paint ing*? The rabbit, not the duck?

Is the power of the flag—and the power, therefore, of a painting paradin as a flag, or of a flag rendered as a painting—an indictment of the present weak ness of the world? In a text titled "The Age of the World Picture" and publishe in 1938—at a time, that is, when he was still a card-carrying member of the Na party, whose heavy-handed symbolism he had been so easily swayed by—th German philosopher Martin Heidegger pointedly asked:

> What is a world picture? . . . . The world picture would be a painting, so to speak, of what is as a whole. But "world picture" means more than this. We mean by it the world itself, the world as such, what is, in its entirety, jus as it is normative and binding for us. "Picture" here does not mean some imitation, but rather what sounds forth in the colloquial expression, "We get the picture" [literally, we are *in* the picture concerning something . . . . Hence world picture, when understood essentially, does not mean a picture of the world but the world conceived and grasped *as* picture.[24]

This goes some way toward explaining Heidegger's inordinate estimation, s deeply rooted in the German philosophical tradition, of the work, as in the *labo* of art. Indeed, Heidegger concludes with a dramatic flourish: "The fundamer tal event of the modern age"—the age of flags, of nations, of modern art an modern artisthood—"is the conquest of the world as picture."[25] And nothin quite captures the idea of conquest as boldly and brazenly as the simple act c *planting*—painting—a *flag*.

⚐22 Værslev's profound investment in these seemingly mundane matters of manufacture aligns his work with that of the still relatively little-known coterie of early-1970s French avant-garde painters grouped under the Support/Surface banner, a major point of comparison and reference in my prior engagement with Værslev's work (see note 12). As I put it in my essay "Version" back in 2017, "Stubbornly, indeed quasi-myopically committed to grasping the medium's true 'material' conditions—these were the late 1960s after all, the high-water mark of historical materialism's popular appeal—these artists primarily focused on painting's underlying structural binary, the coupling of which gave the group its name: Support/Surface. The collective's glory years stretched from 1966 to 1974, during which time they appeared in numerous self-organized exhibitions (often in the most unlikely locales) and published a journal titled, rather grandiosely, *Peinture: Cahiers théoriques*, noted for its highly politicized, manifesto-style language and predilection for dour doctrine. Indeed, revisiting the work made under the Support/Surface banner today, it is somewhat hard to imagine the Maoist fervor and militancy that animated the making of so much of it, whether it be the surface-centric 'paintings' of Claude Viallat, Jean-Pierre Pincemin, Louis Cane and André-Pierre Arnal (all of whom worked, in one way or other, with unstretched canvas) or the support-focused 'paintings' of Daniel Dezeuze, Toni Grand or Bernard Pagés (all of whom worked, in one way or other, with wooden stretcher bars)." Dieter Roelstraete, "Version," 114. Looking back at the Support/Surface legacy today and taking particular note of the preference of some of these artists for working with unstretched, sagging, or casually draped canvas, I am struck by the absence of any overt references to the art of the flag in this corpus. Perhaps flags were simply on too many people's minds, for obvious political reasons, to be taken seriously as paintings. On the art historically related matter of authorial mark making, see the influence on Værslev's work of an associated French artist collective partly contemporaneous with Support/Surface, namely the foursome composed of Daniel Buren, Olivier Mosset, Michel Parmentier, and Niele Toroni (BMPT for short), another frame of reference amply alluded to in the aforementioned essay. Of the four, Buren in particular made the most expansive use of the flag as a painterly medium, most notoriously in his *Peinture-Sculpture* (08), a ten-meter-wide, thirty-meter-long striped banner that was hung from the skylight of the Guggenheim Museum in New York in 1971, obscuring the work of artists like Dan Flavin and Donald Judd also on view at the time. The latter, of the doctrinaire minimalist conviction that "painting is something you back into when you want to look at a sculpture," complained that Buren's "painting-sculpture" blocked views of his work from the rotunda's spiraling staircase, and the Guggenheim ultimately decided to remove it, laying the groundwork for one of institutional critique's founding myths in the process, as well as for the persistent "problem" of flag art: those pesky flying objects that obstruct our view of "real" art.

⚐23 In an email to the author, Værslev relayed how one of the "triggers" that helped shape his decision to spend close to two full years of his life making paintings of something as generic and seemingly exhausted as flags is the fact that, *as flags*, they are all "wrong"—a matter, most prosaically, of deliberate disregard for the demands of proportion so integral to the logic of standardization. While all of Værslev's *World Paintings* are the same size (theirs is the all-purpose horizontalism of some Platonic idea of landscape painting, alluding to the entwinement of "flag" and "land," of national identity and terrain or *terroir*), this is of course not true of the flags they mimic. This gentle act of sabotage is most apparent in Værslev's US flag, whose top and bottom red bands are much wider than the red and white bands between them, for the simple reason that the painted canvas is allowed to wrap around the frame, effectively disqualifying the painting as a proper flag in the process. *Phew!* They are *paintings* after all. *Rabbits*.

⚐24 Martin Heidegger, "The Age of the World Picture" (1938), in *The Question Concerning Technology and Other Essays*, trans. William Lovitt (New York: Harper and Row, 1977), 129. This was the first text to be published by Heidegger after the publication, two years prior, of his epochal *The Origin of the Work of Art*. Together, both texts delineate the high-water mark of the philosopher's engagement with (visual) art, ominously coinciding with the zenith of the Third Reich's aesthetic achievement. The period from 1936 until 1938 was when art mattered most to failed Sunday painter Adolf Hitler. The Nazis obviously knew a thing or two about the pageantry of politicized togetherness. See for instance the infamous Nuremberg rallies and Berlin Olympics of 1936, the source for so much of our culture's lingering unease when facing the "problem" of flag art. In his essay from 1938, Heidegger proposes the following as part of his attempt to distill the essence of the modern age—that of the "world picture": "a third equally essential phenomenon of the modern period lies in the event of art's moving into the purview of aesthetics. That means that the art work becomes the object of mere subjective experience." Heidegger, "The Age of the World Picture," 116.

⚐25 Heidegger, "The Age of the World Picture," 116.

08

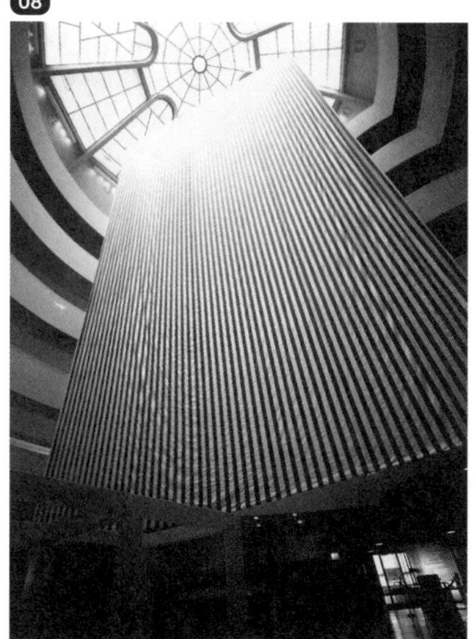

● Illustration in Joseph Jastrow, “The Mind’s Eye,” *Popular Science Monthly*, 54 (1899): 299–312.

01 David Hammons, *African-American Flag*, 1990. © 2020, The Museum of Modern Art, New York / Scala, Florence. Promised gift to The Museum of Modern Art and The Studio Museum in Harlem by the Hudgins Family in memory of Jack Tilton

02 Pope.L, *Trinket*, 2015, *William Pope.L: Trinket* installation views at Museum of Contemporary Art, Los Angeles, 2015. © Pope.L. Courtesy: the artist

03 Yevgeny Khaldei, *Raising a Flag over the Reichstag*, May 2, 1945. Photo: User: Каракорум / Wikimedia Commons / CC BY 4.0

04 Joe Rosenthal, *Raising the Flag on Iwo Jima*, February 23, 1945. Photo: User: Bammesk / Wikimedia Commons / CC-0

05 Olle Bærtling, *YIO*, 1977. © Olle Bærtling, by SIAE 2020. Courtesy: Bærtling Foundation and Galerie Nordenhake, Berlin / Stockholm / Mexico City

06 Cady Noland, *Oozewald* (detail), 1989, *Cady Noland* installation view at MUSEUM MMK FÜR MODERNE KUNST, 2019. Photo: Fabian Frinzel

07 Jasper Johns, *Flag*, 1954. © Jasper Johns, by SIAE 2020 / 2020, The Museum of Modern Art, New York / Scala, Florence

08 Daniel Buren, Photo-souvenir: *Painting-Sculpture*, work in situ (detail) in VI Guggenheim International, Guggenheim Museum, New York, February 1971 © Daniel Buren, by SIAE 2020

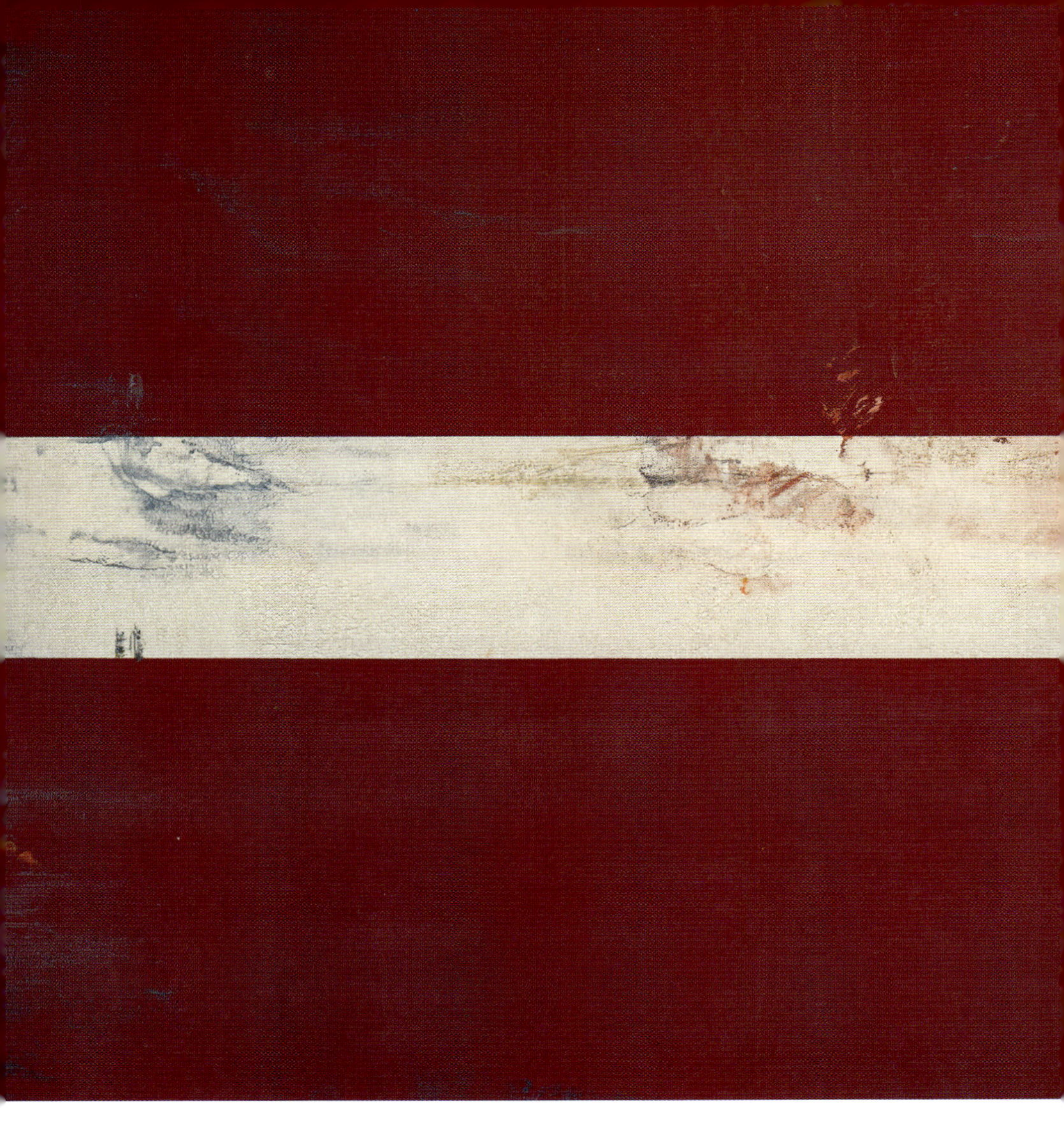

LATVIA

P 74

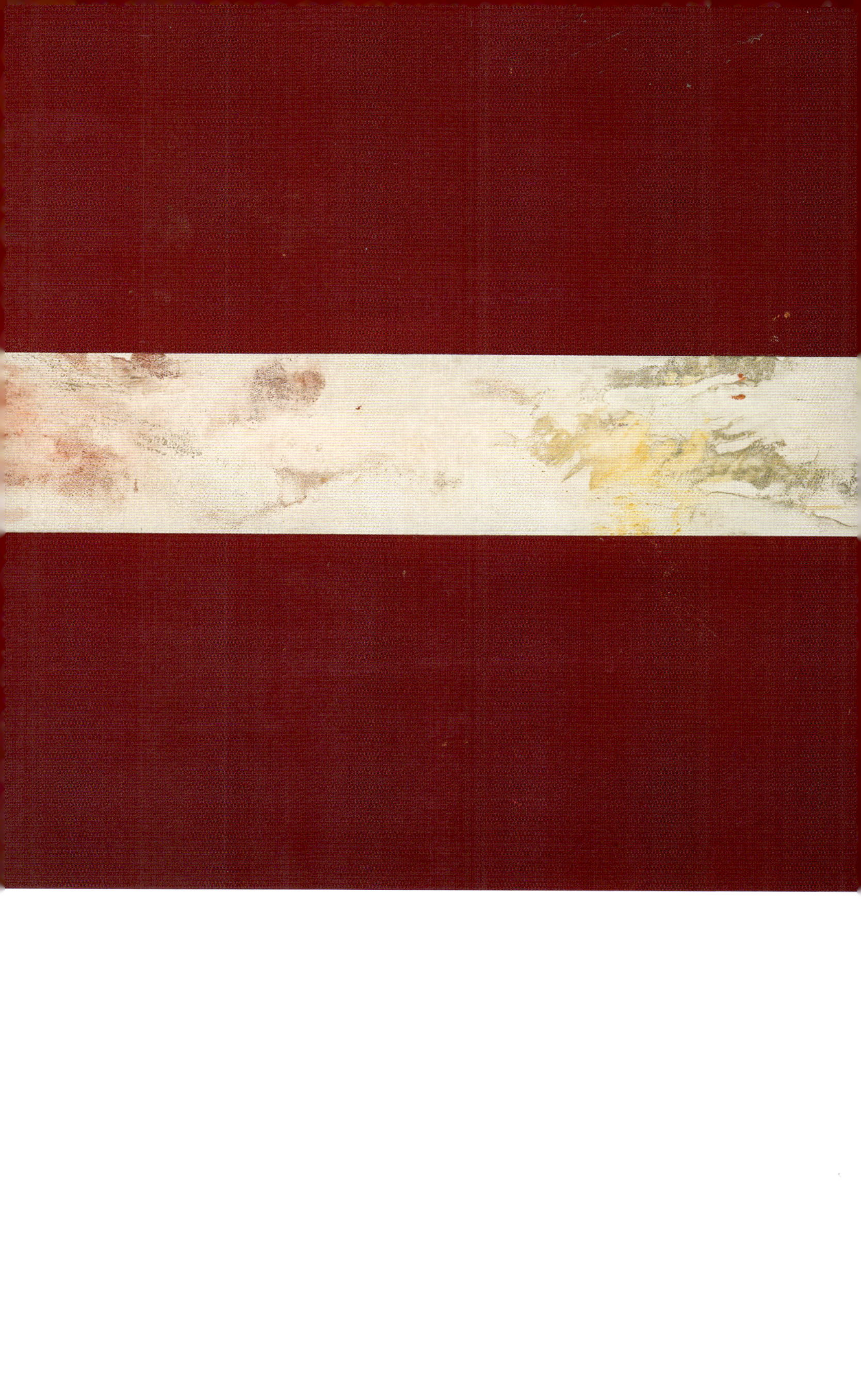

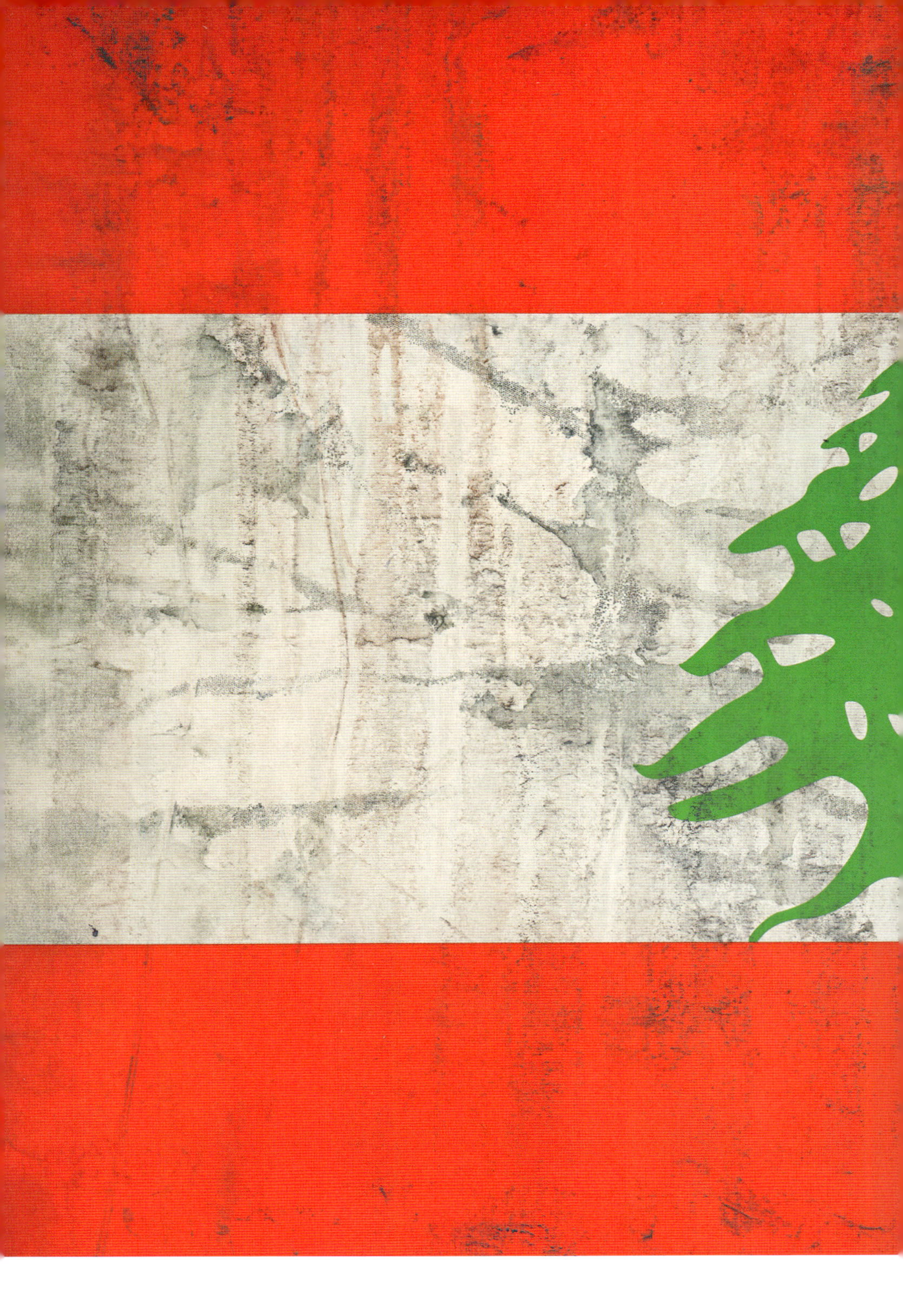

LEBANON

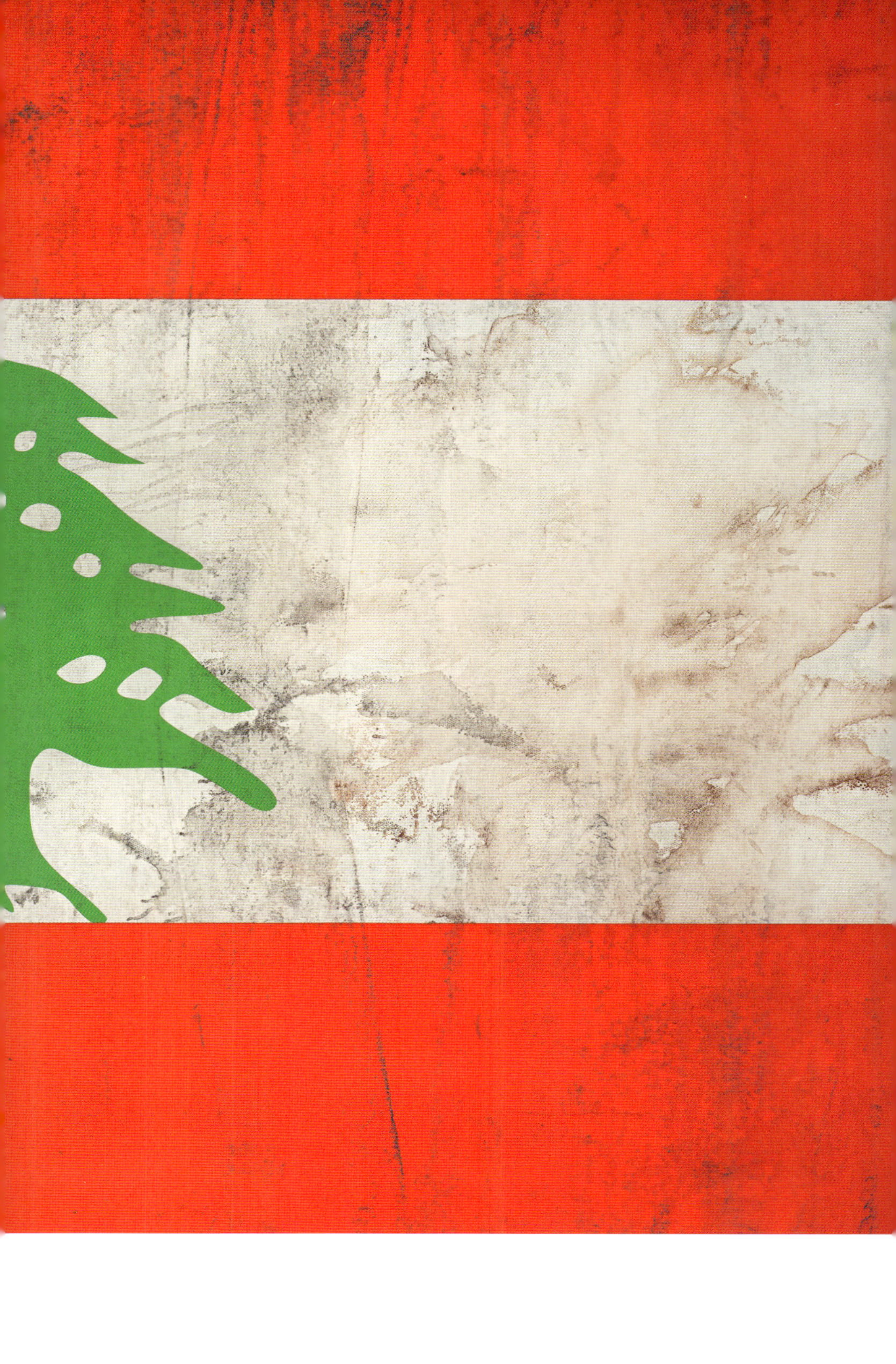

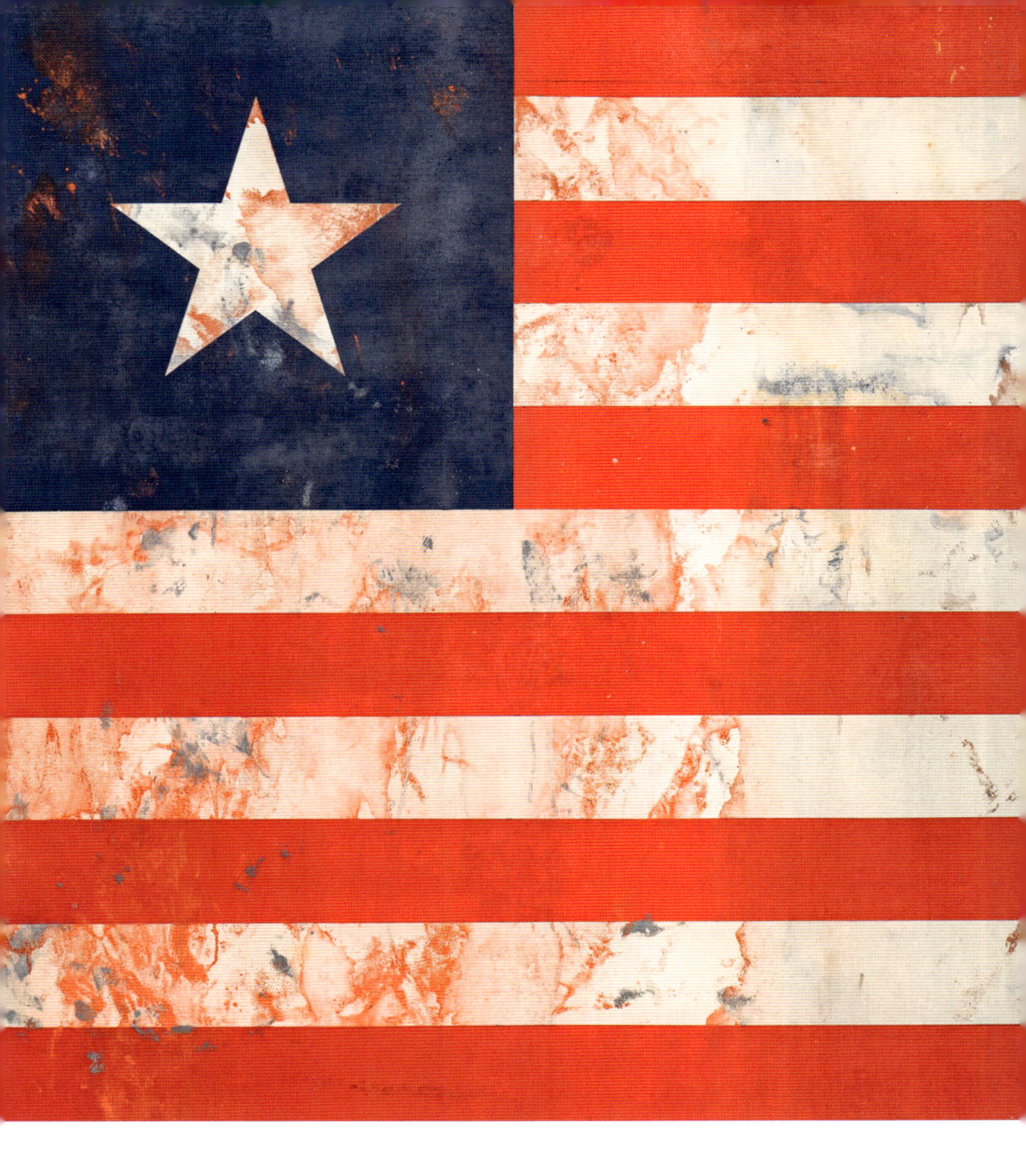

LIBERIA

P 78

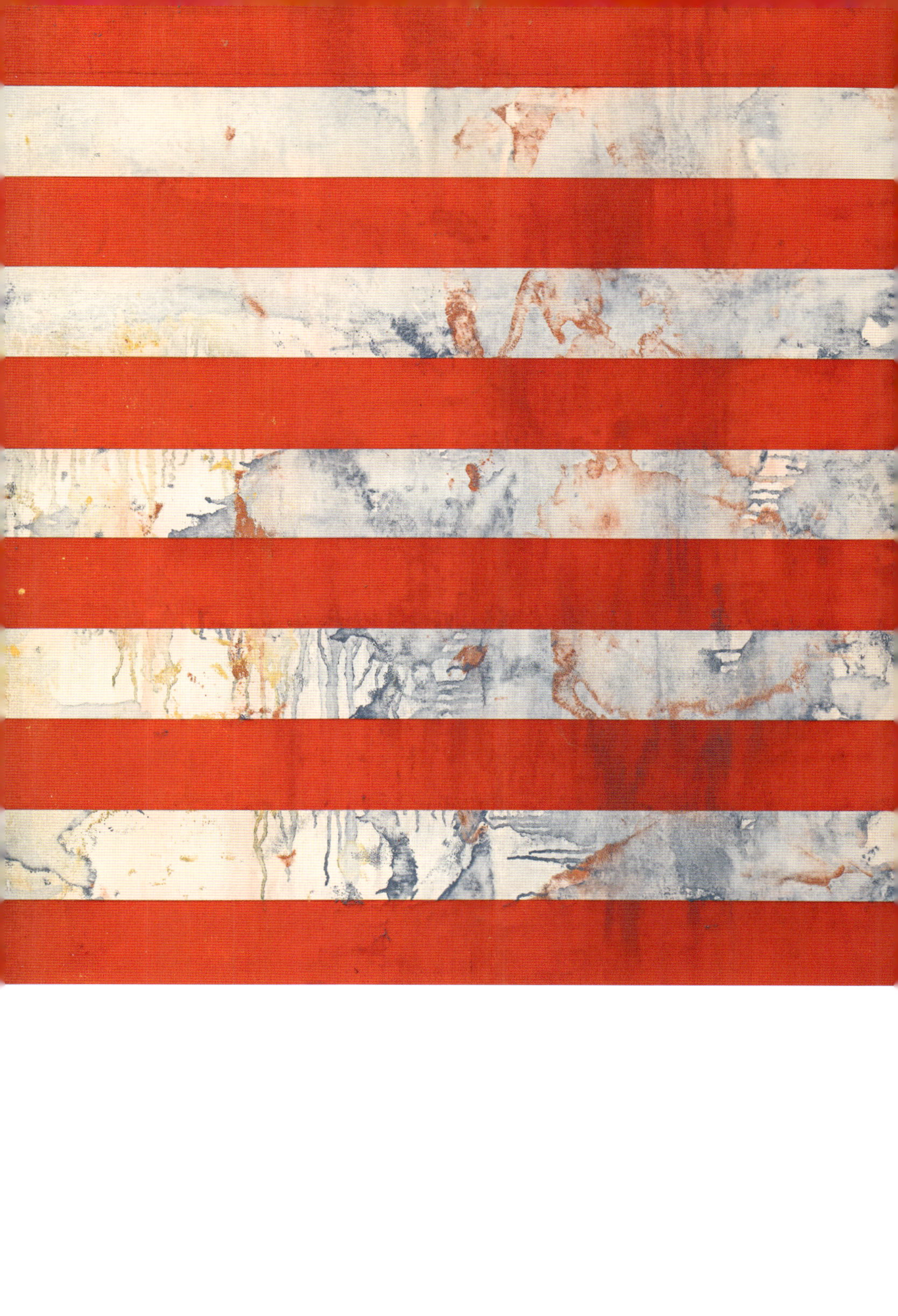

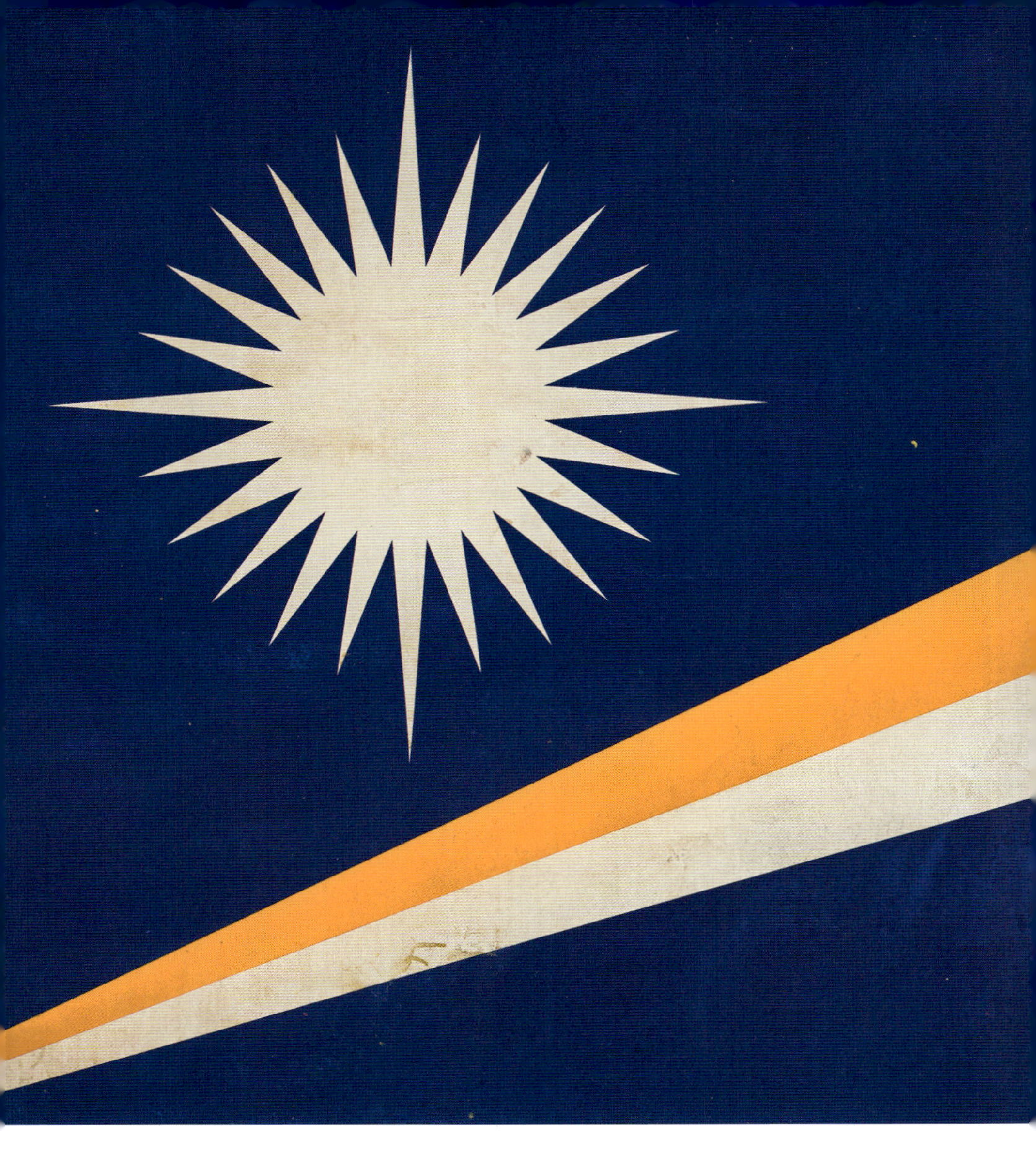

MARSHALL ISLANDS

P 80

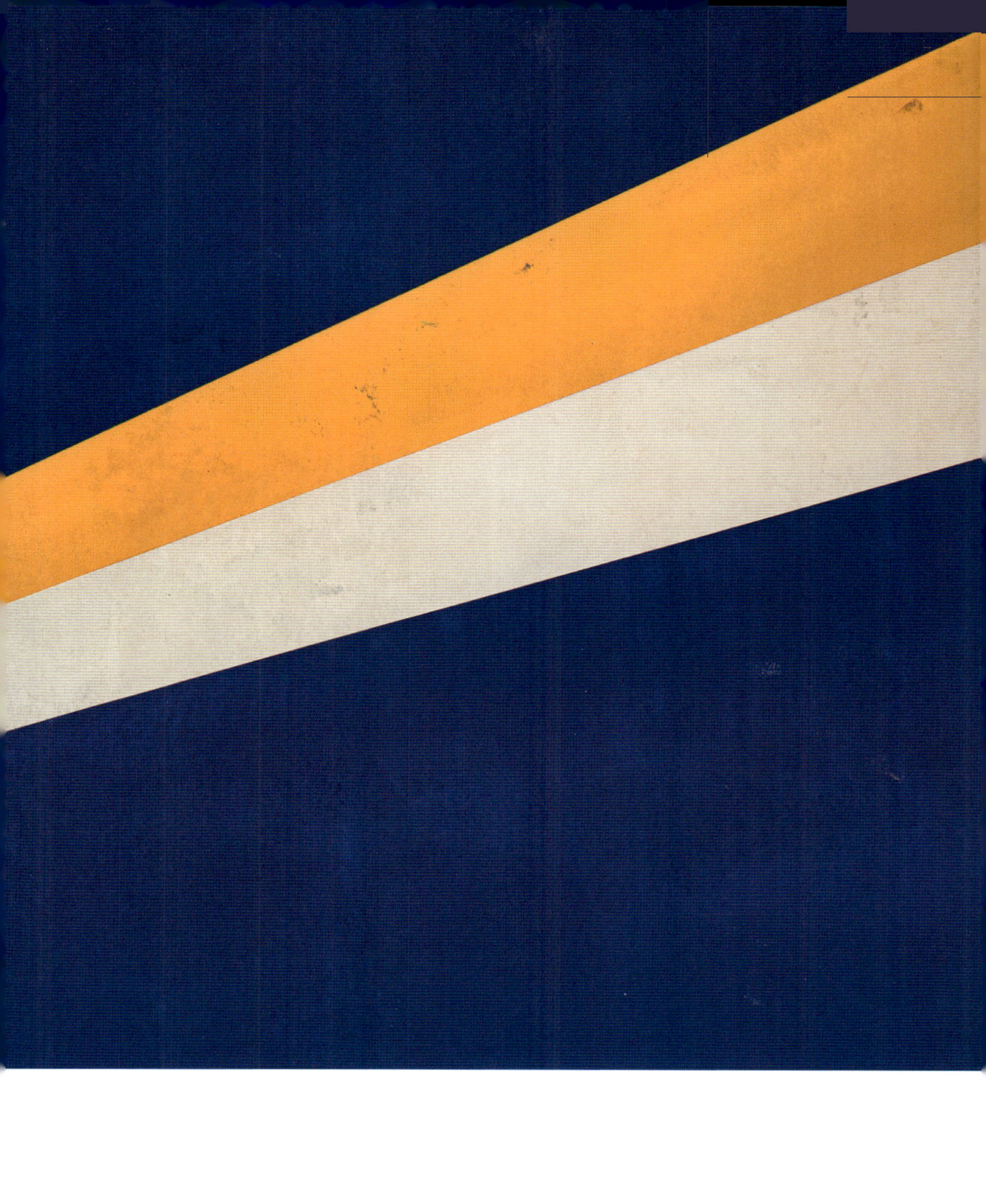

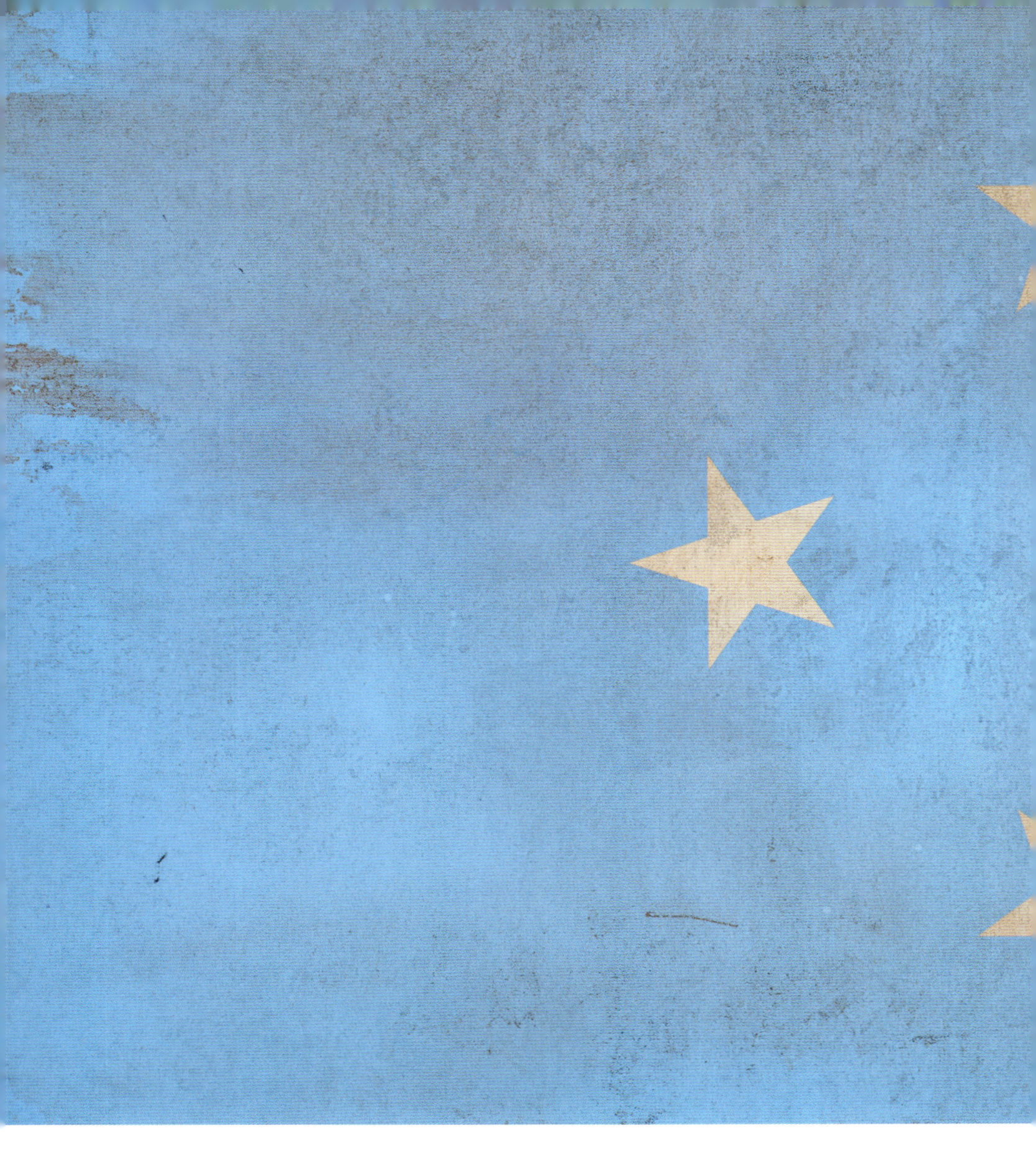

MICRONESIA

P 82

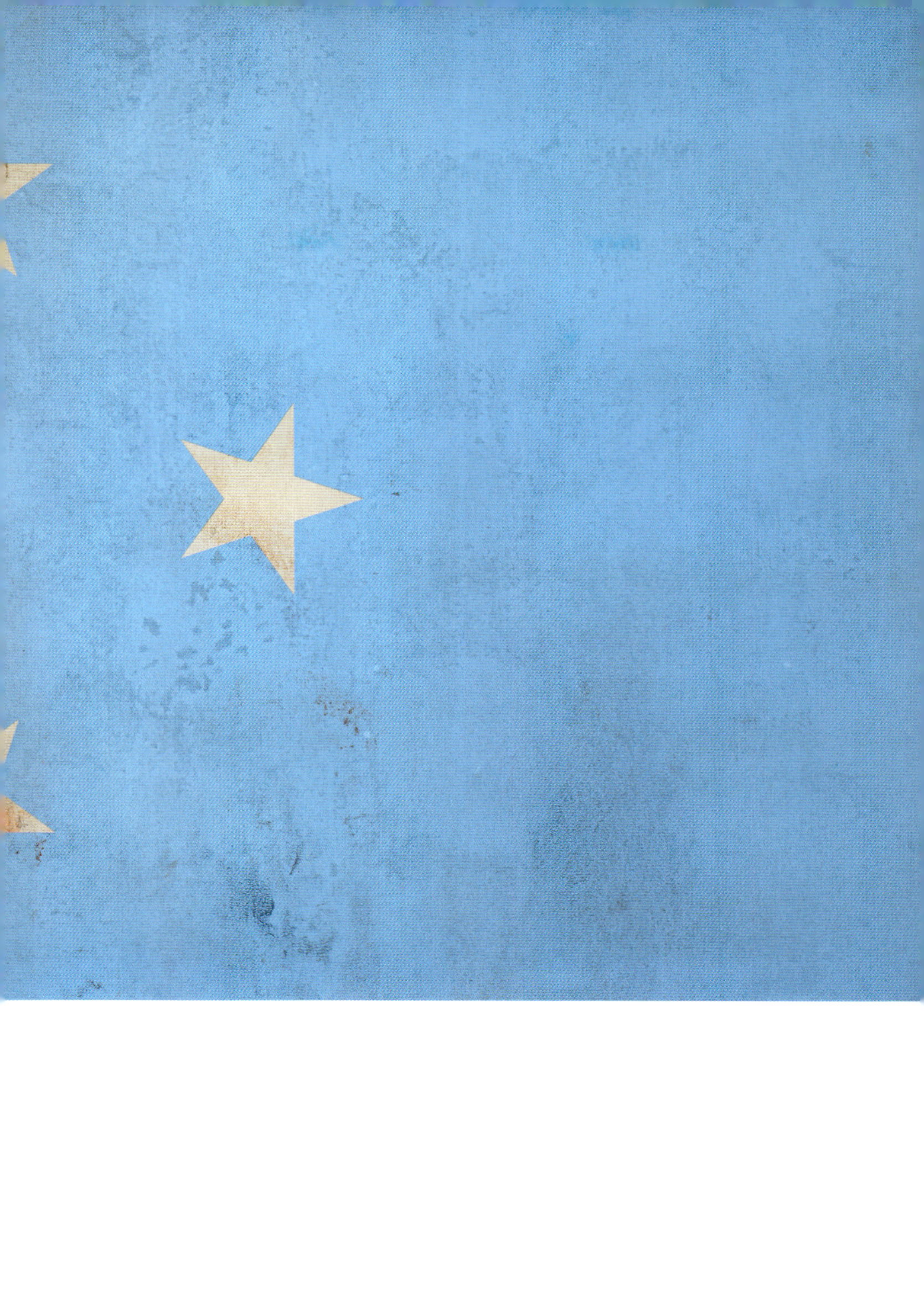

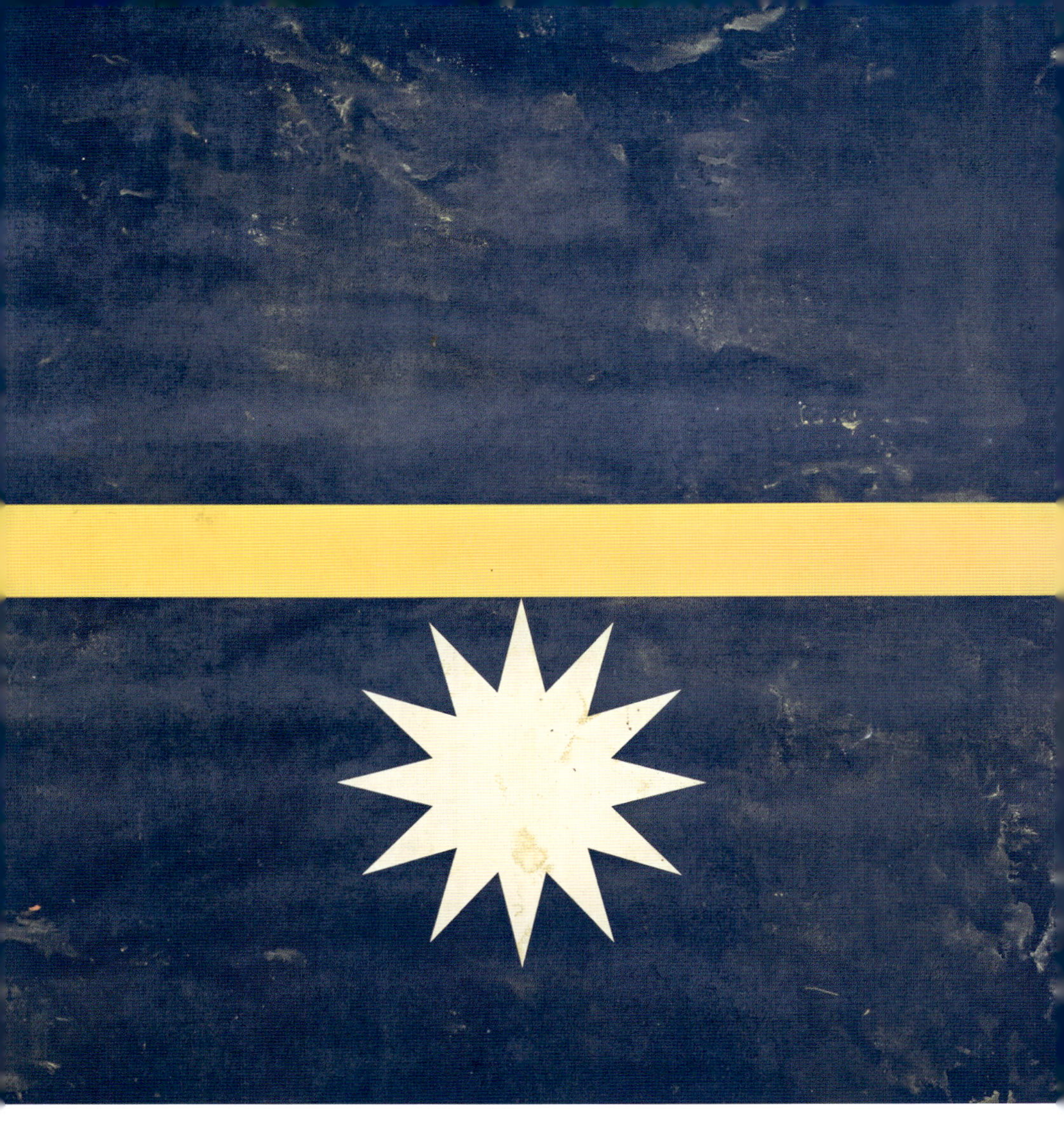

⚑ NAURU

P 84

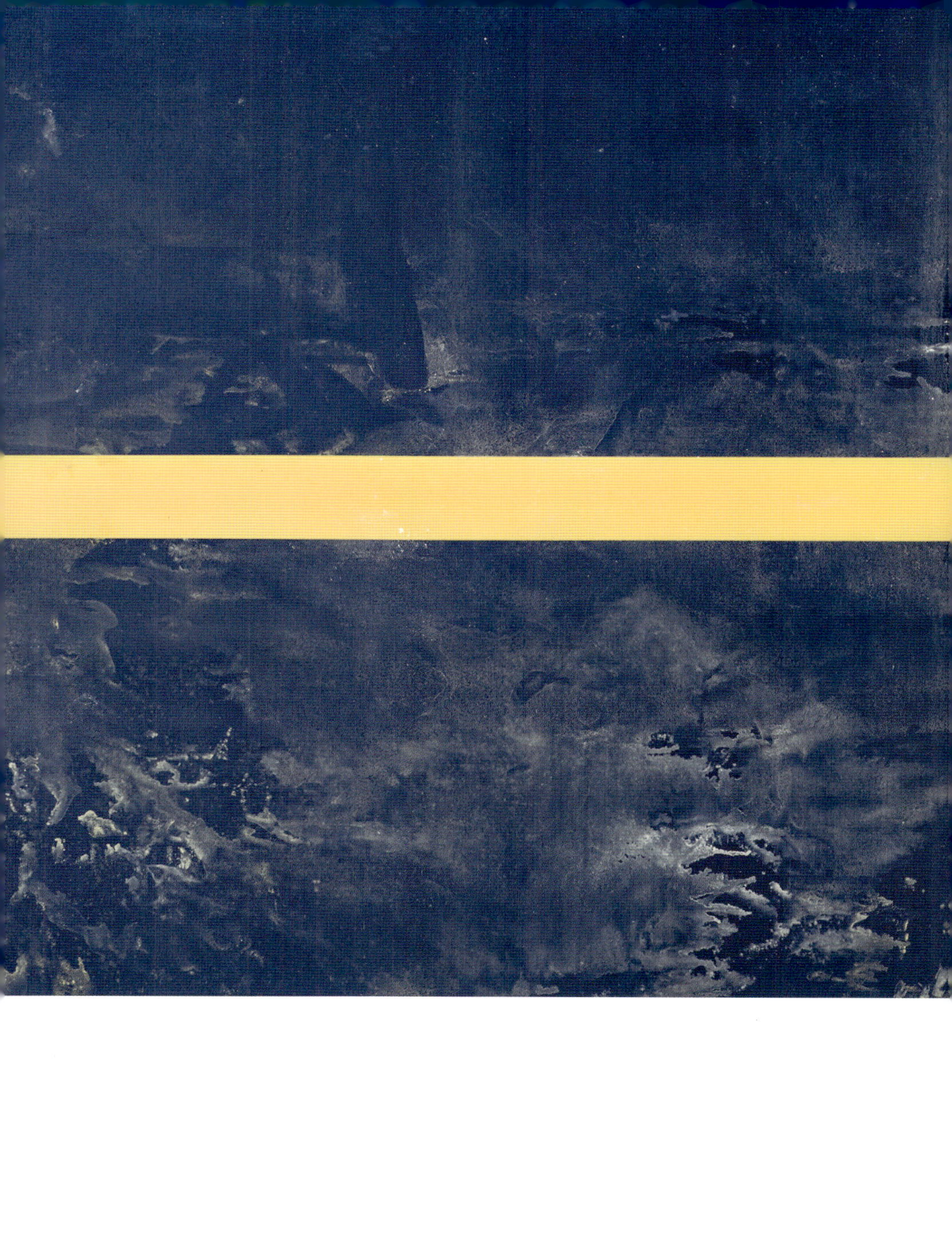

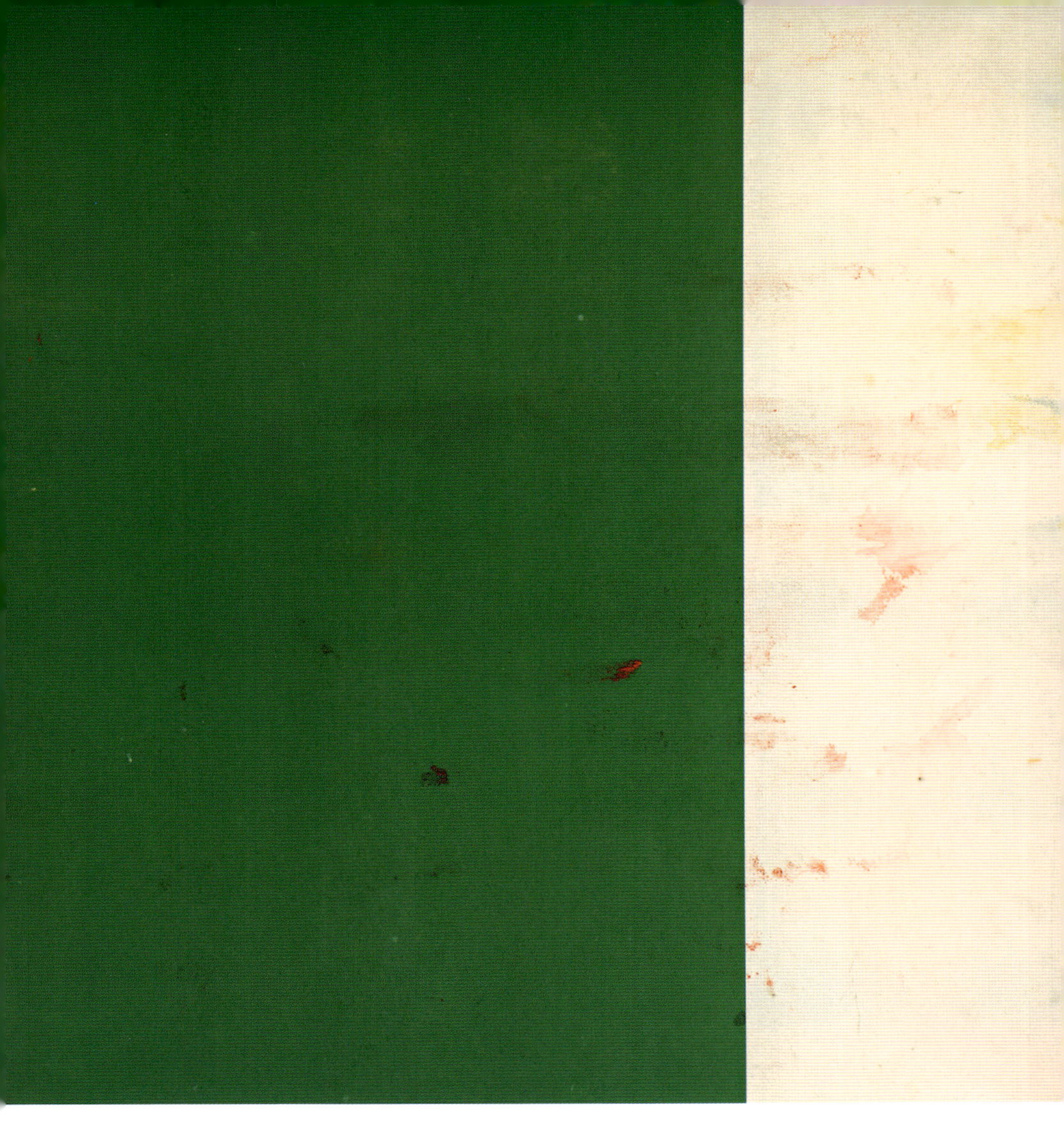

NIGERIA

P 86

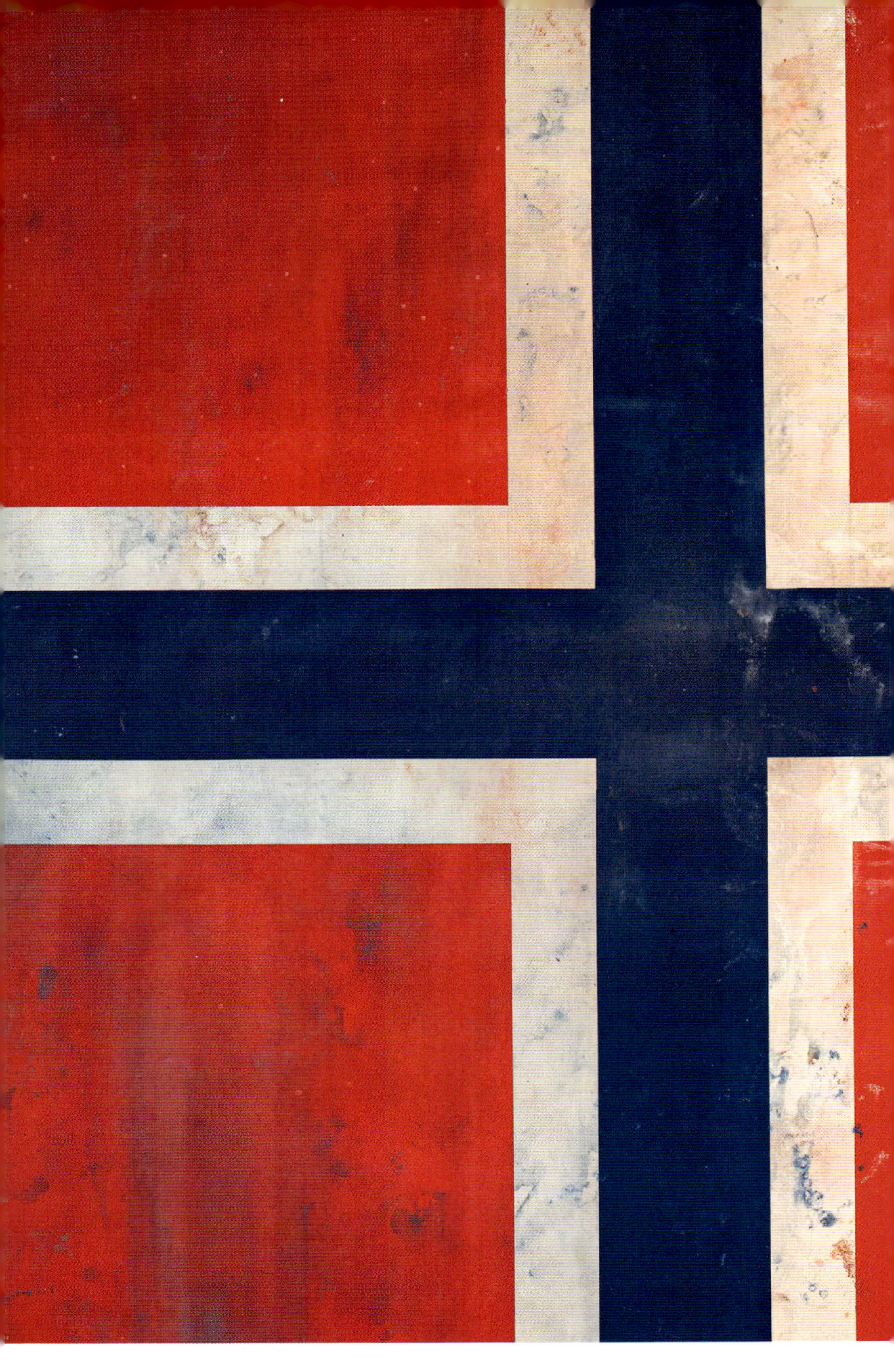

NORWAY

P 88

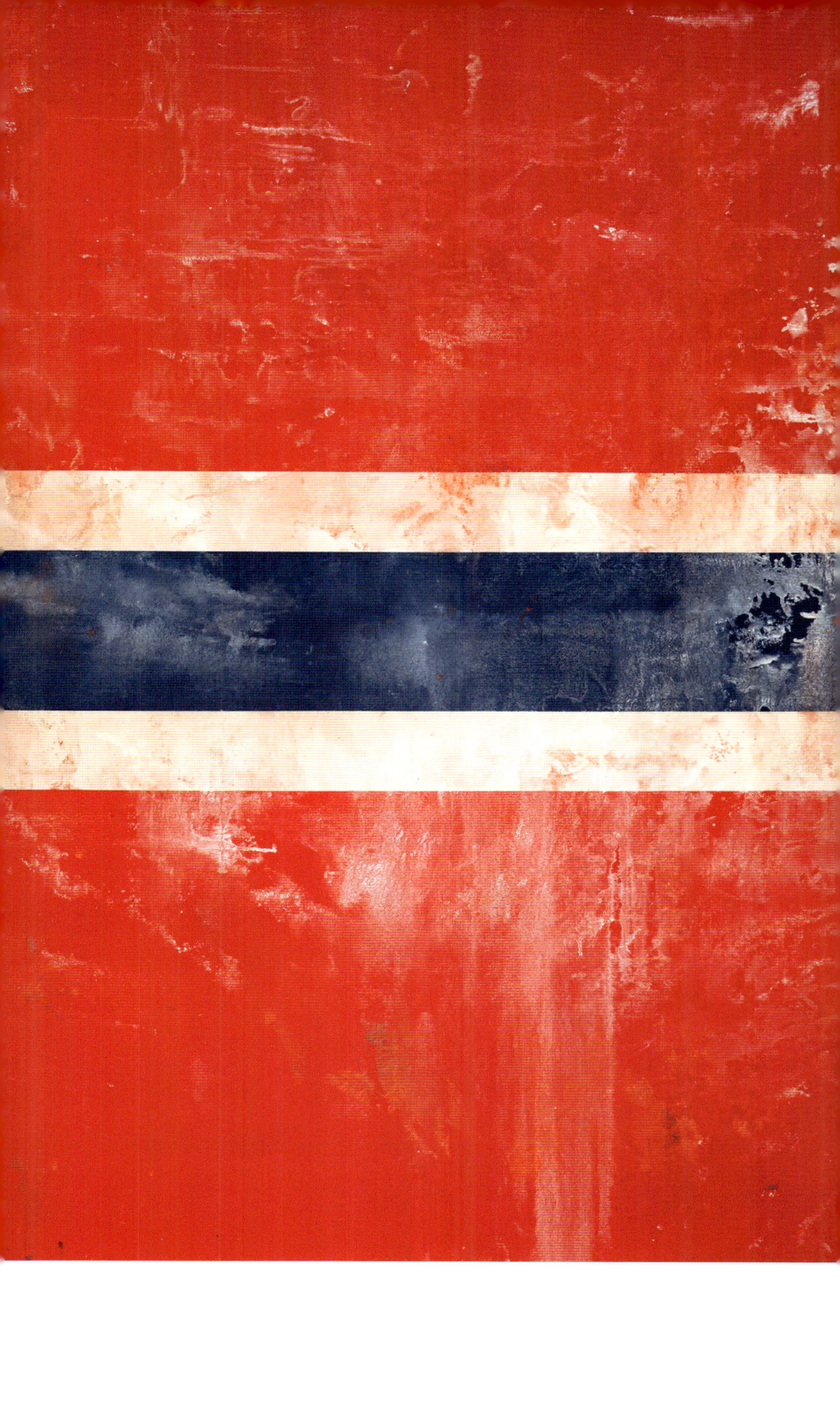

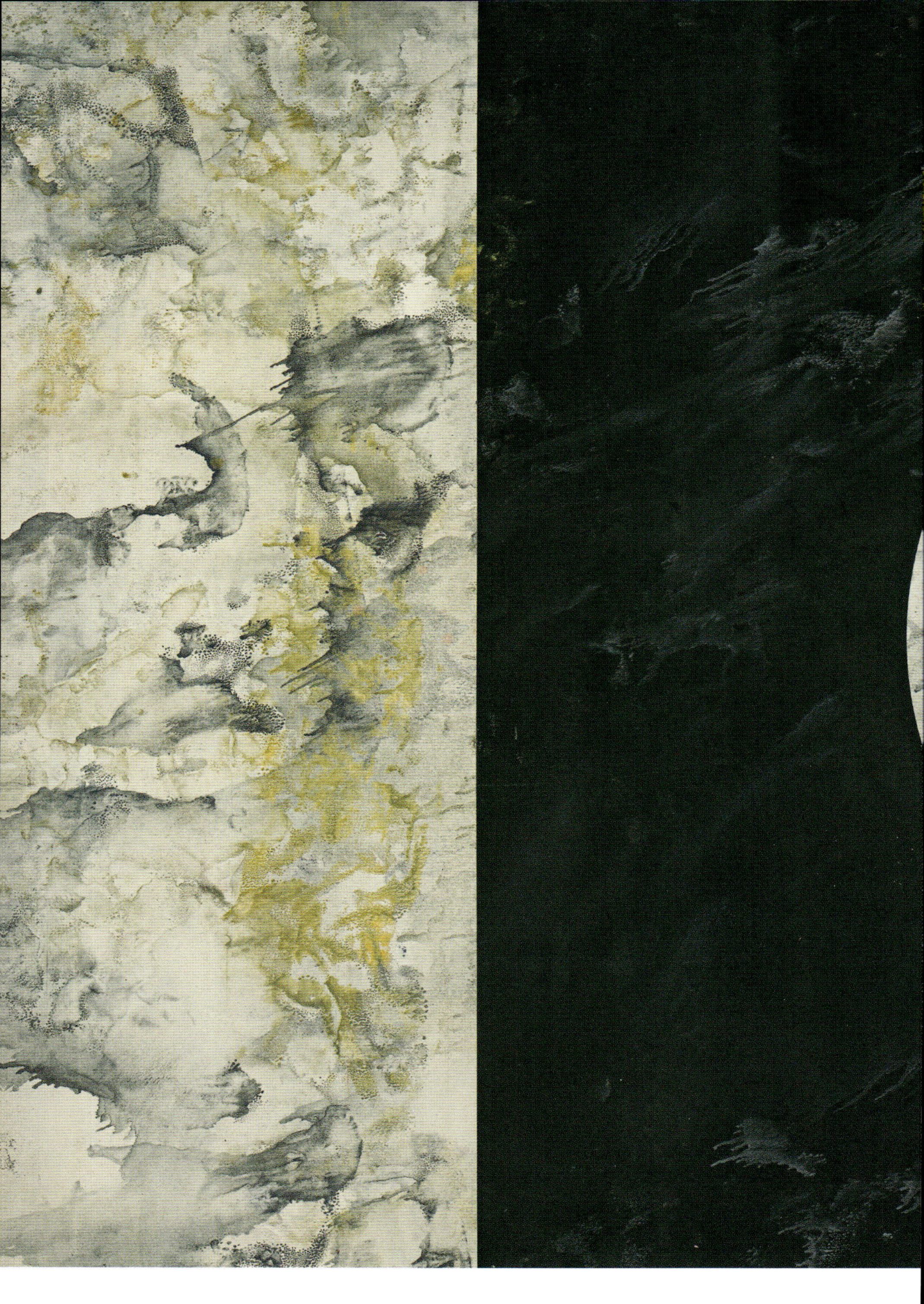

PAKISTAN

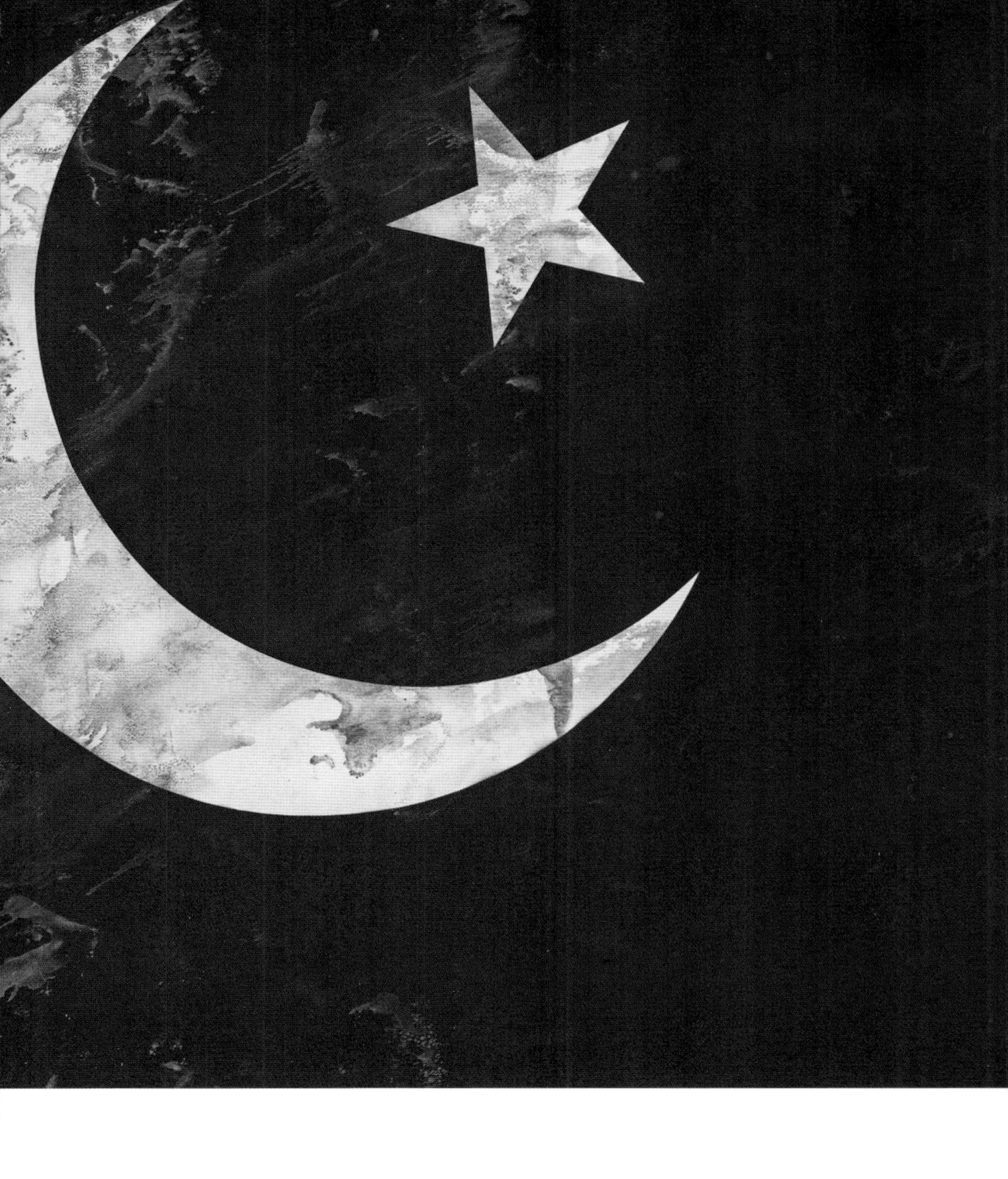

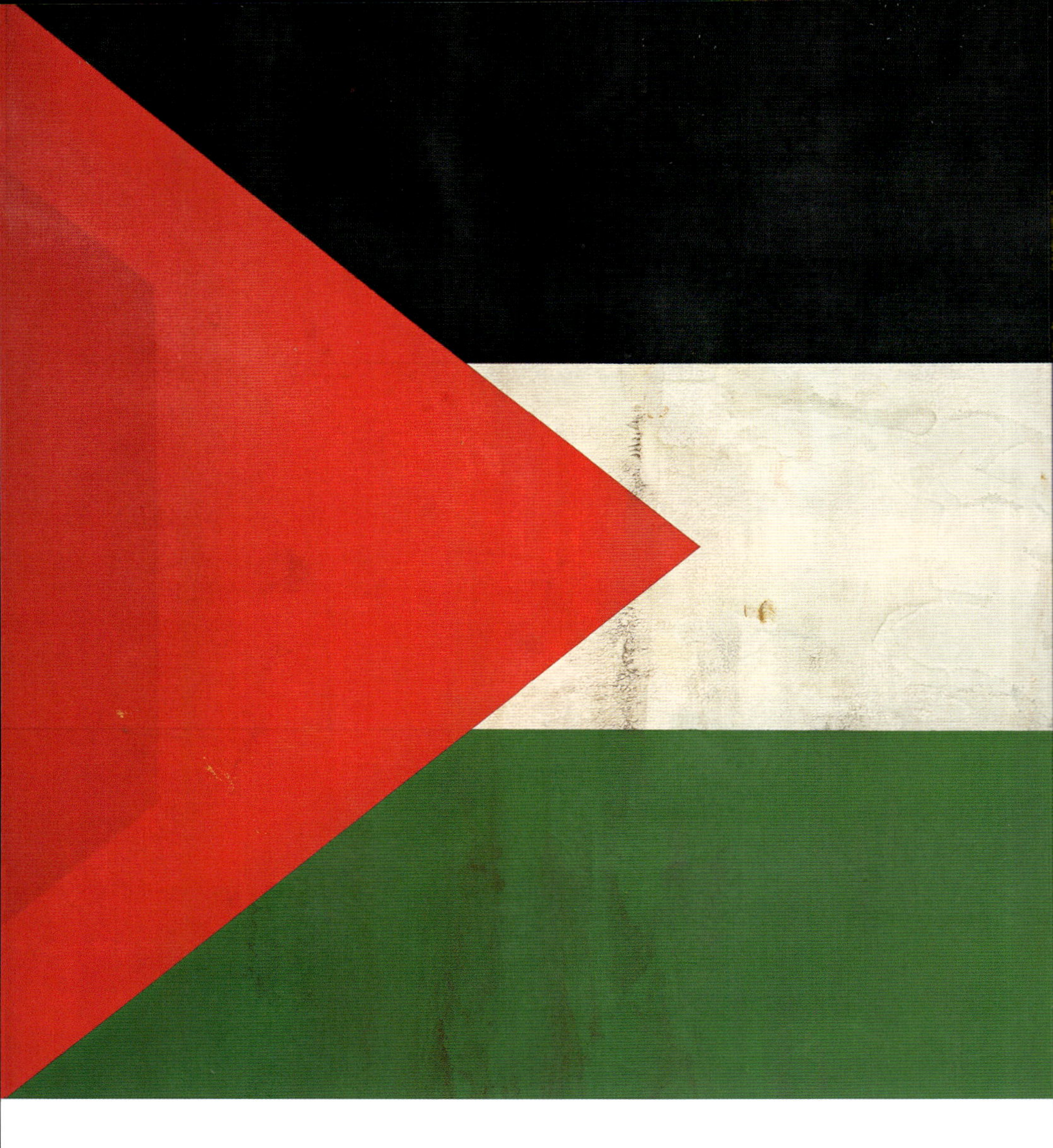

PALESTINE

P 92

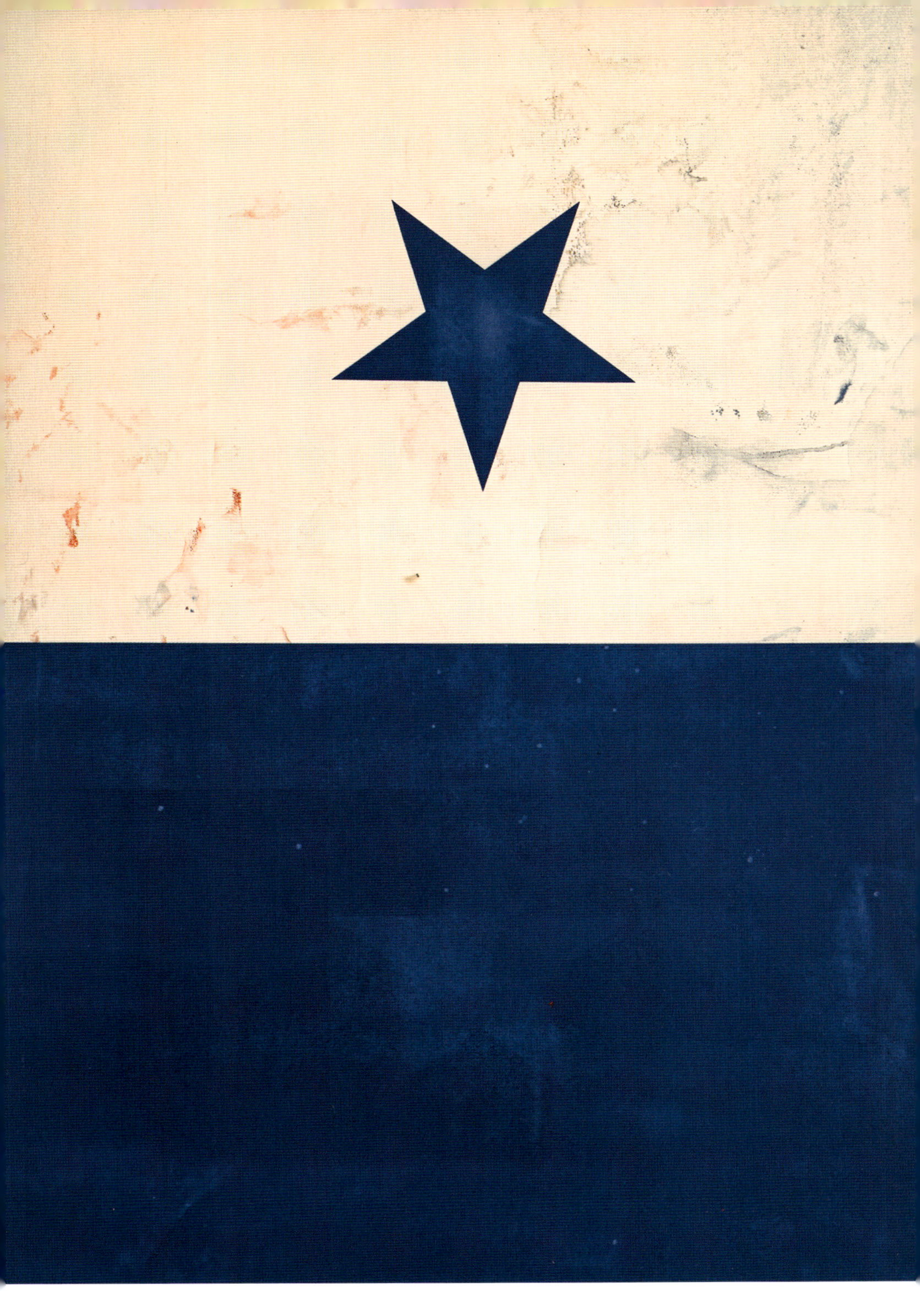

PANAMA

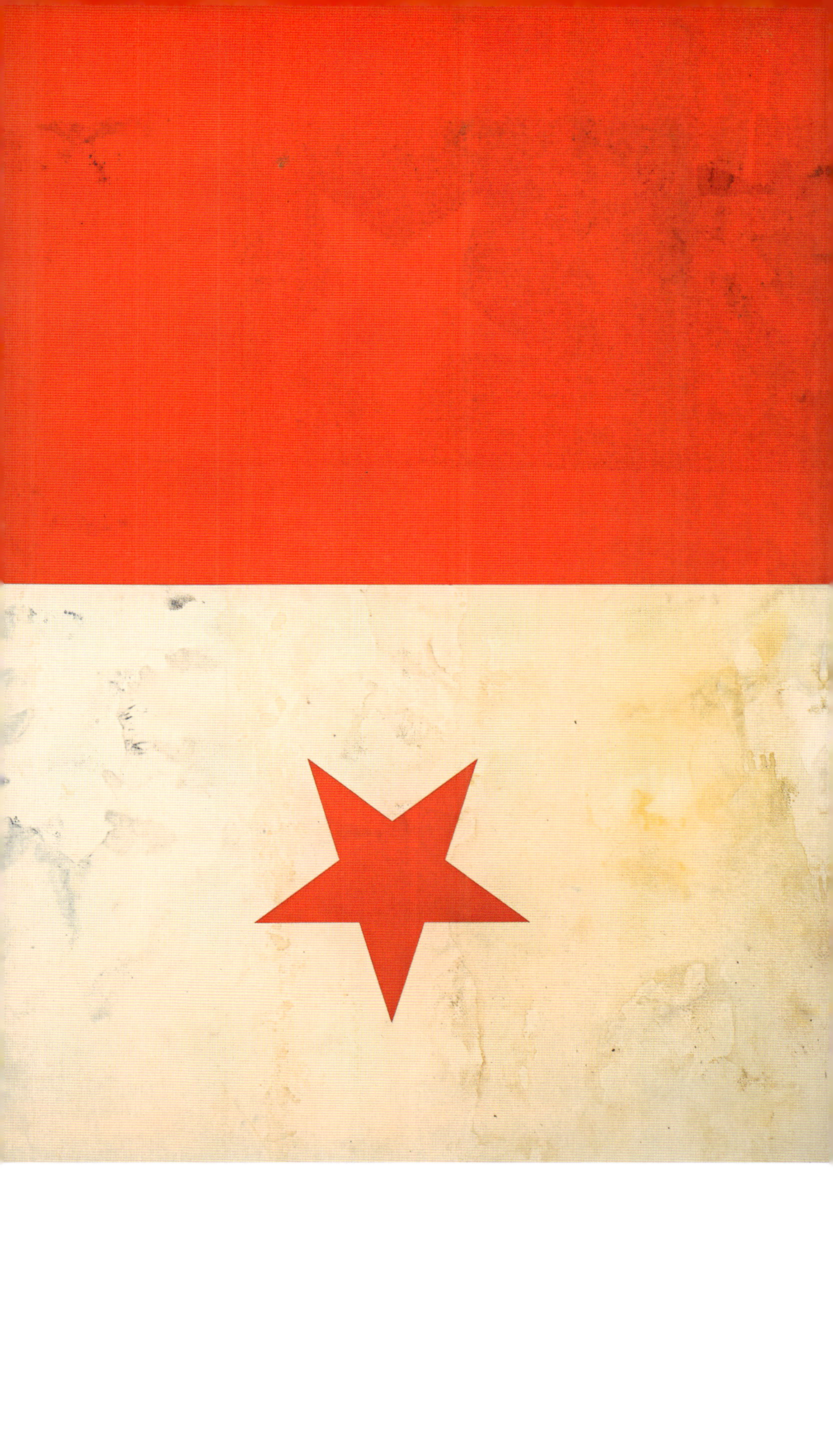

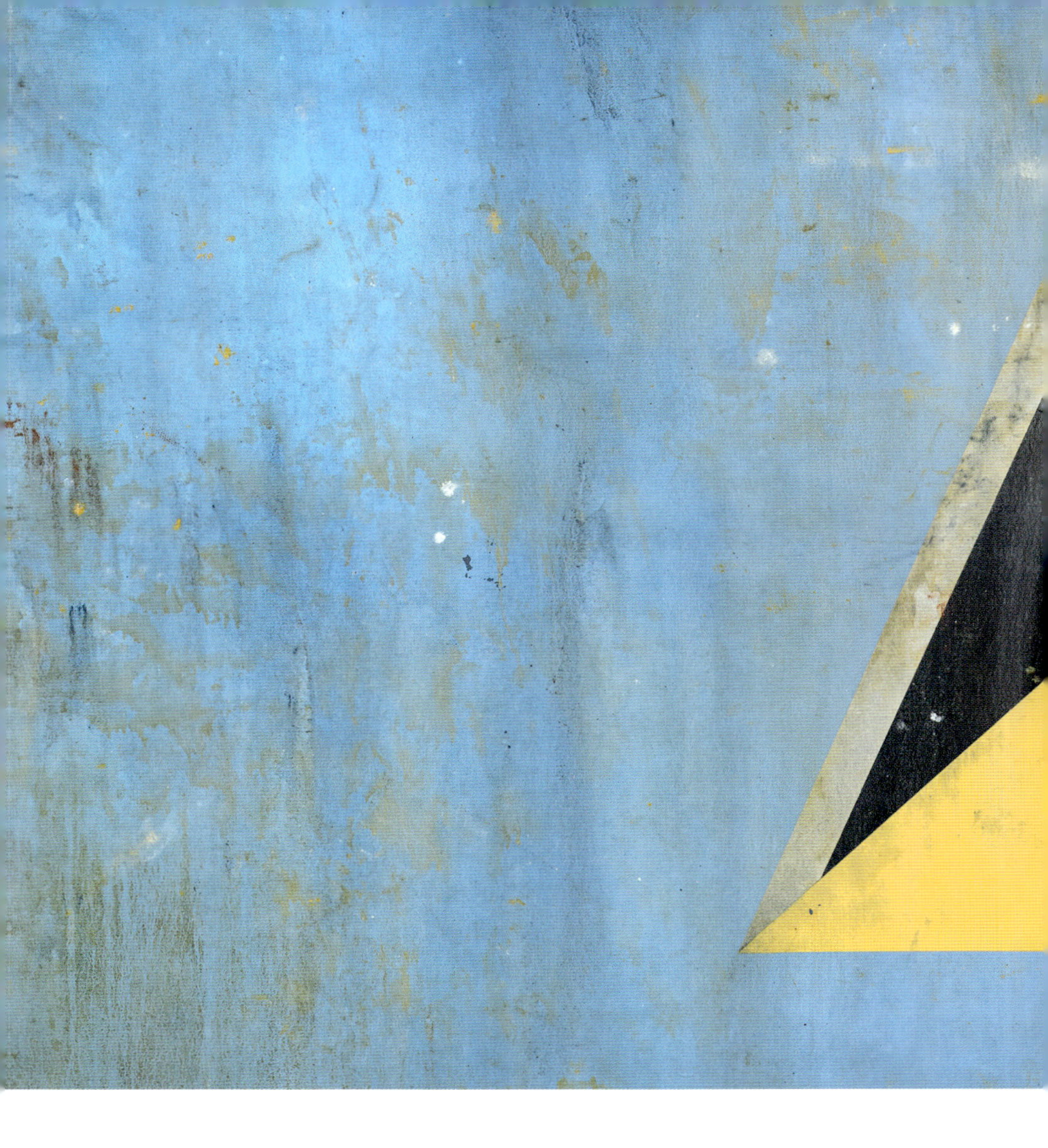

SAINT LUCIA

P 96

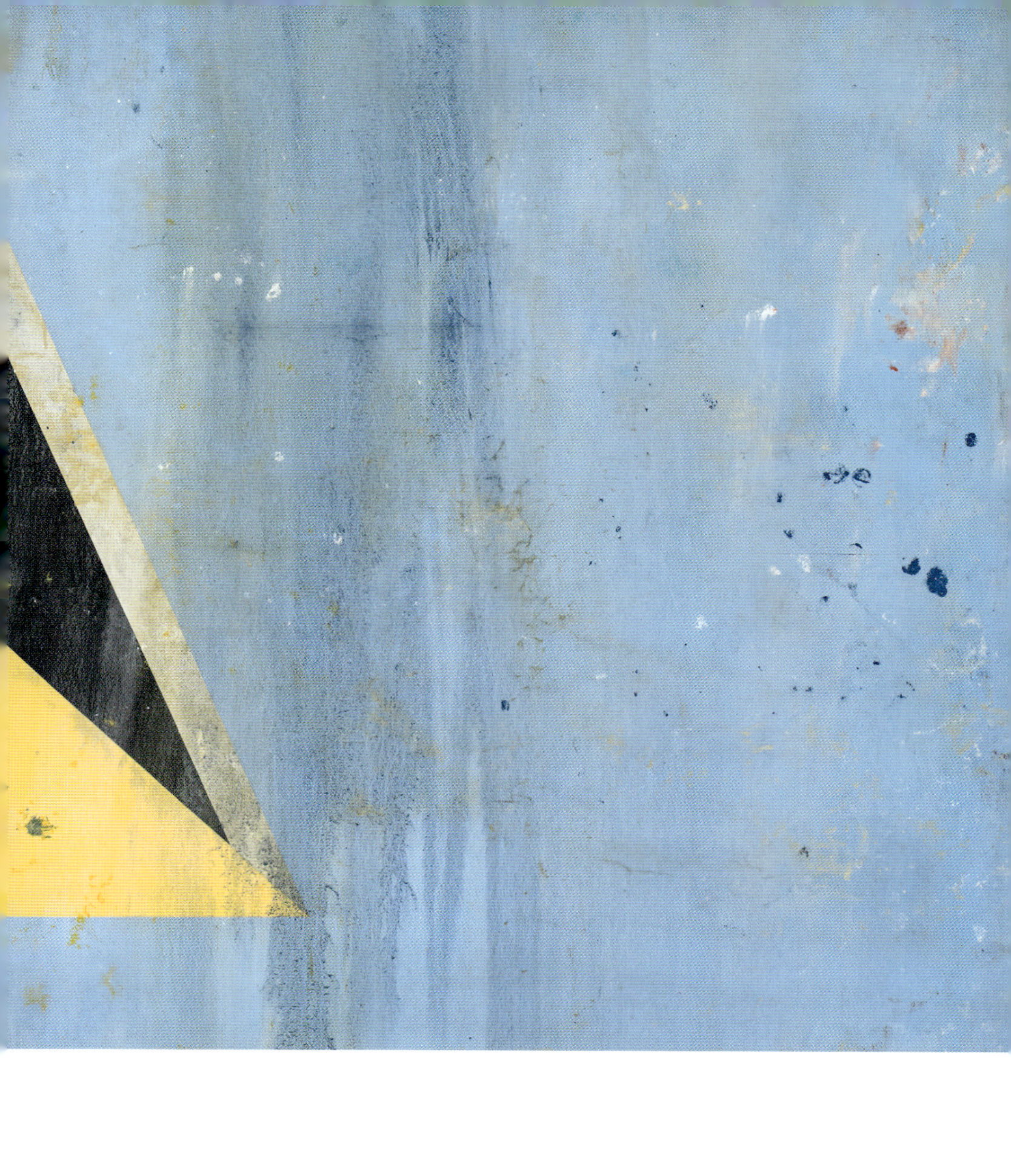

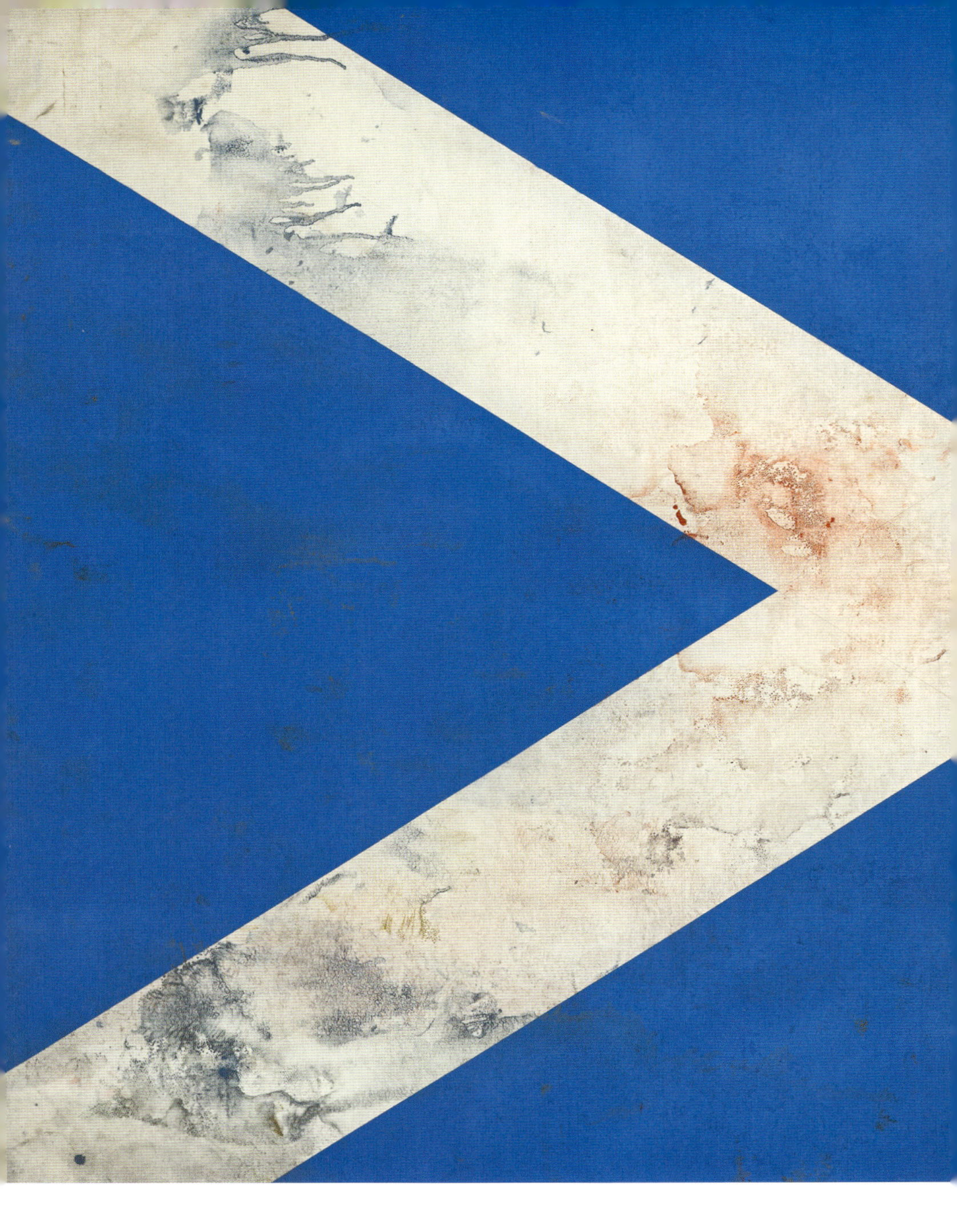

SCOTLAND

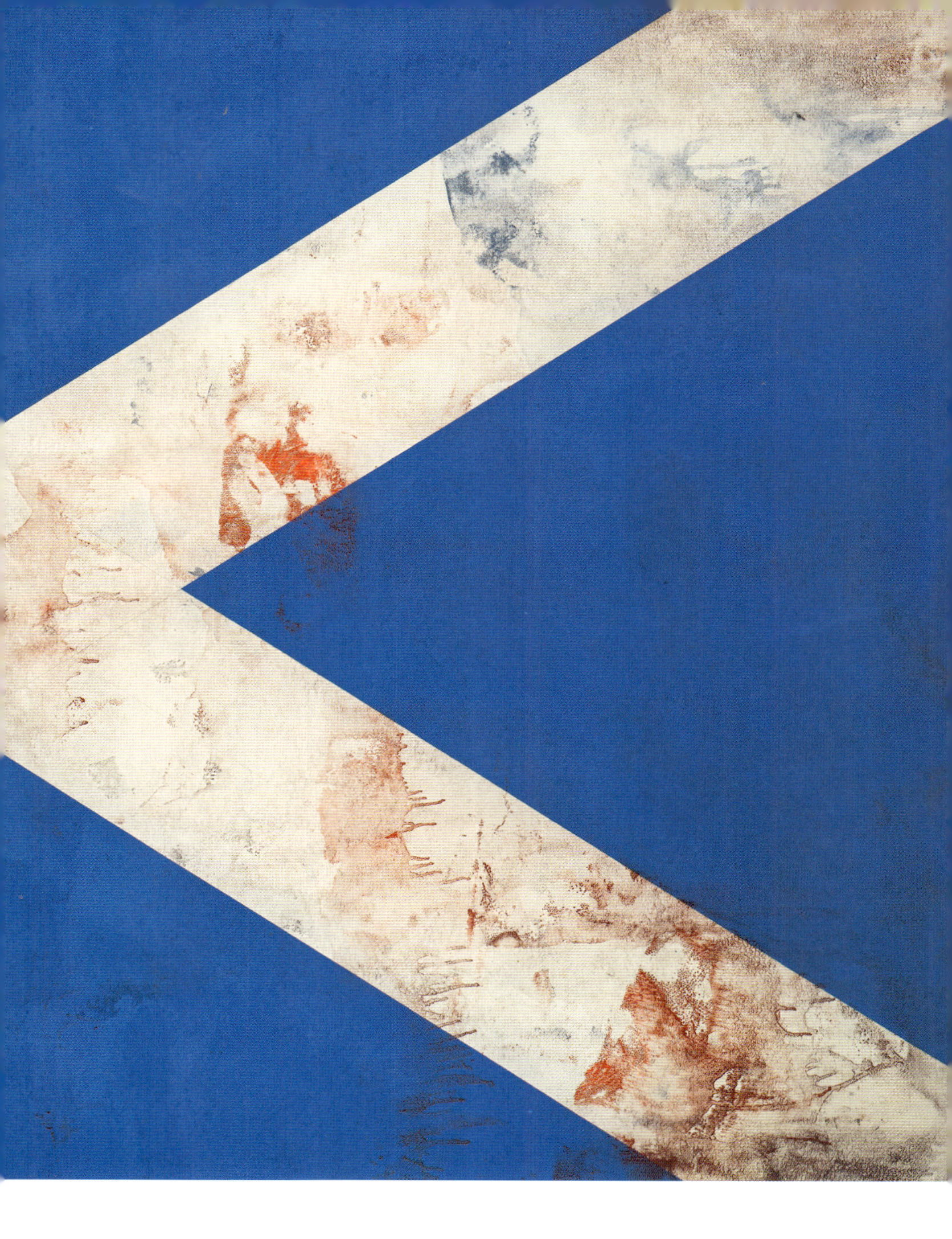

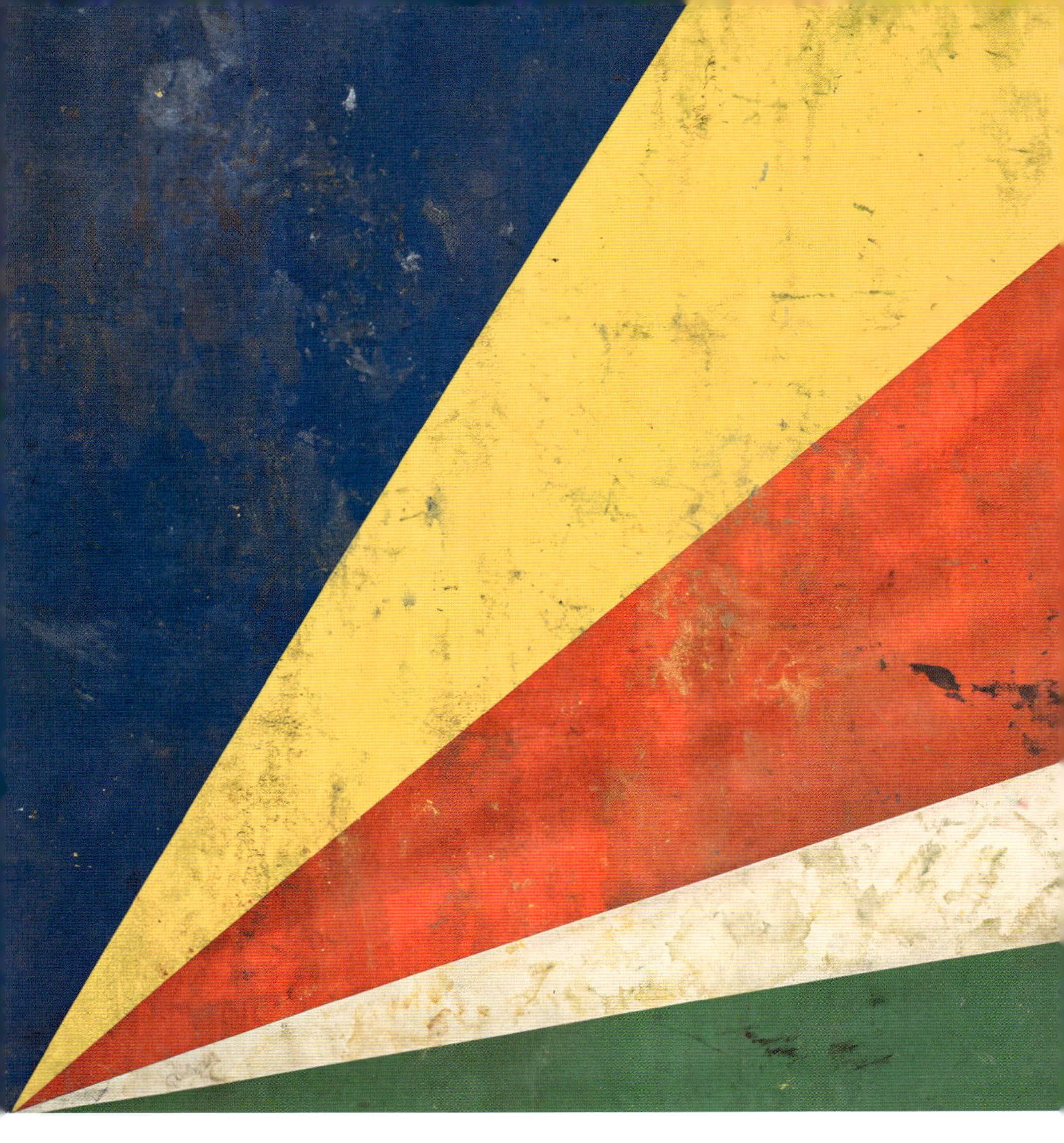

SEYCHELLES

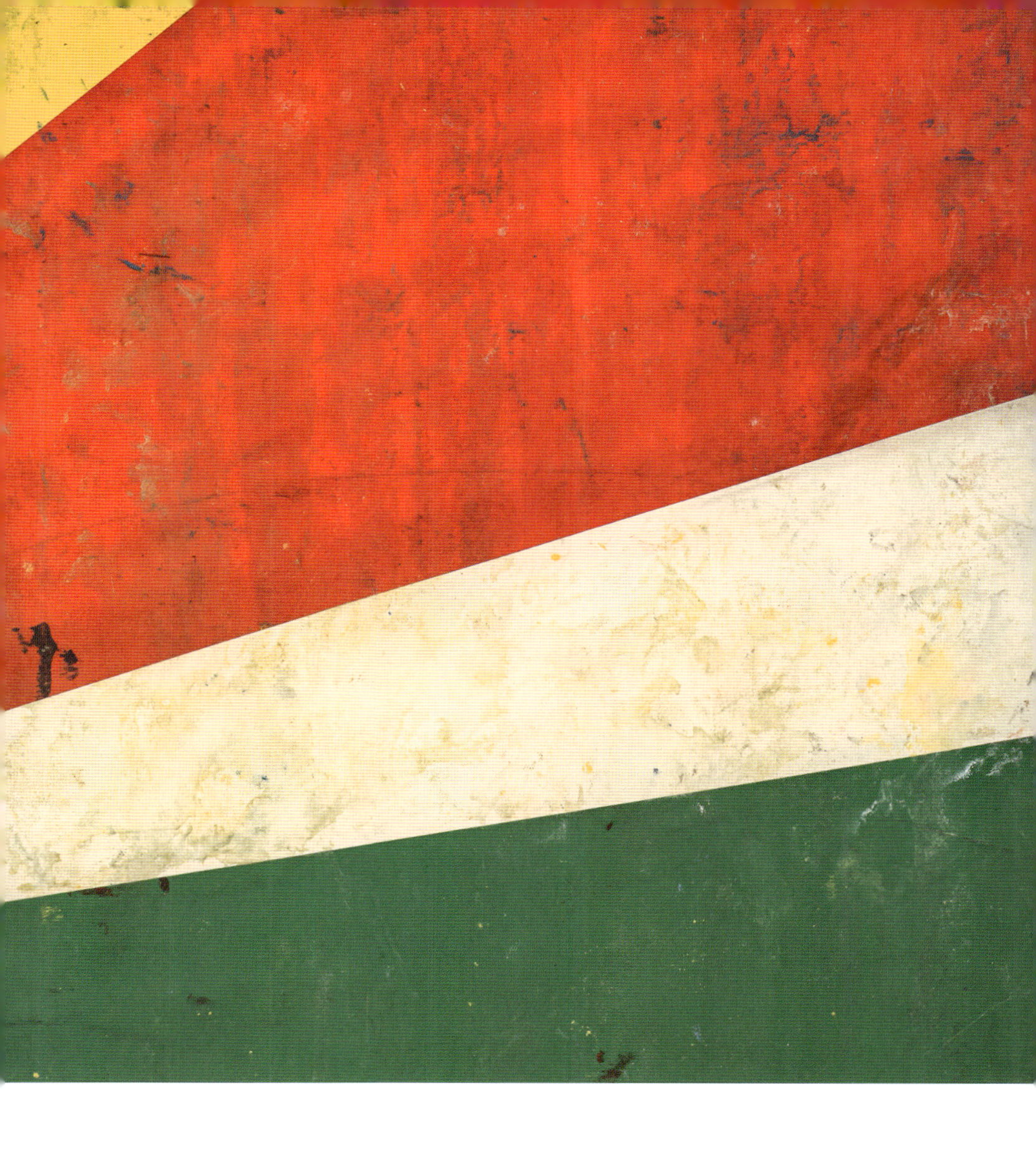

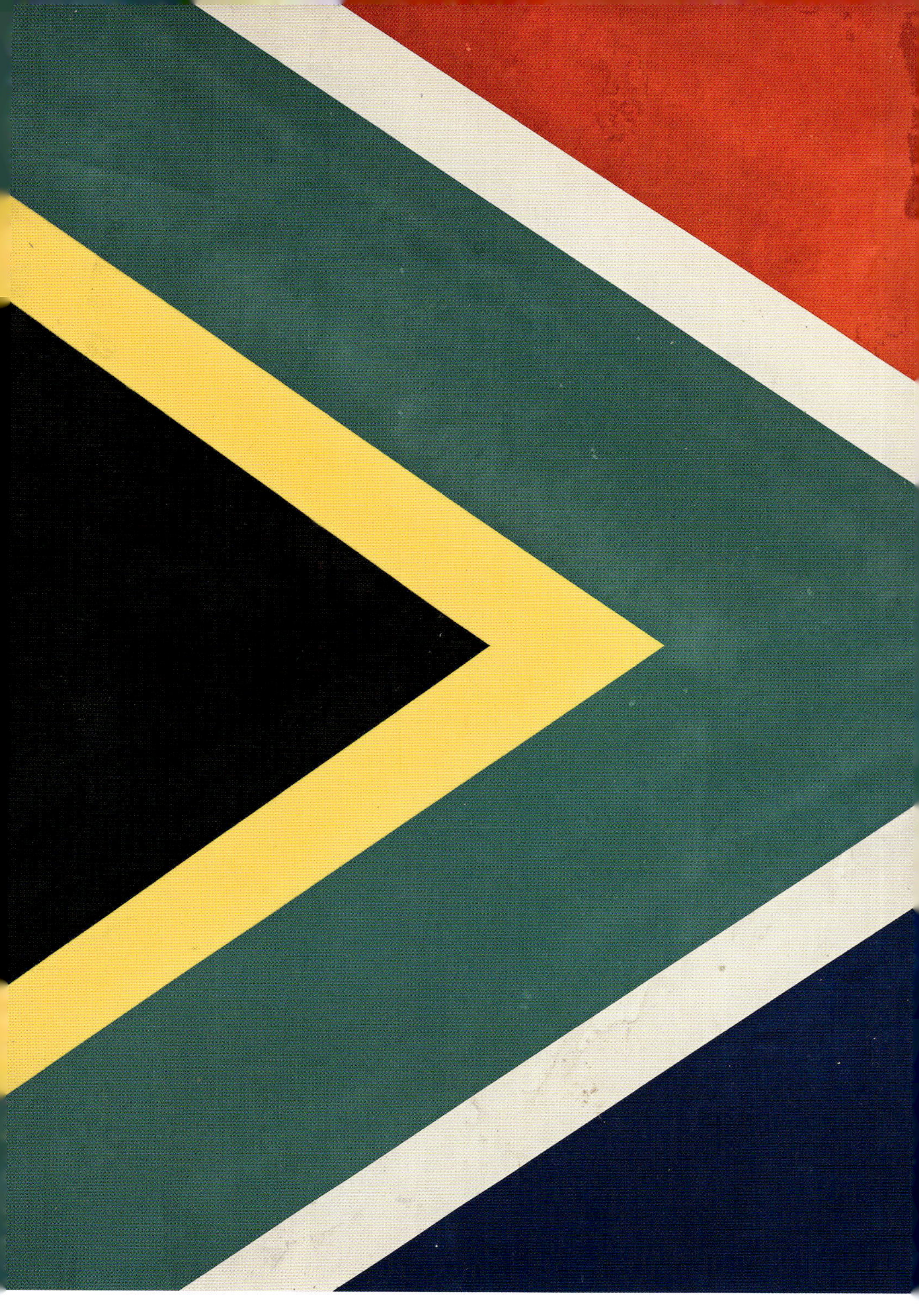

SOUTH AFRICA

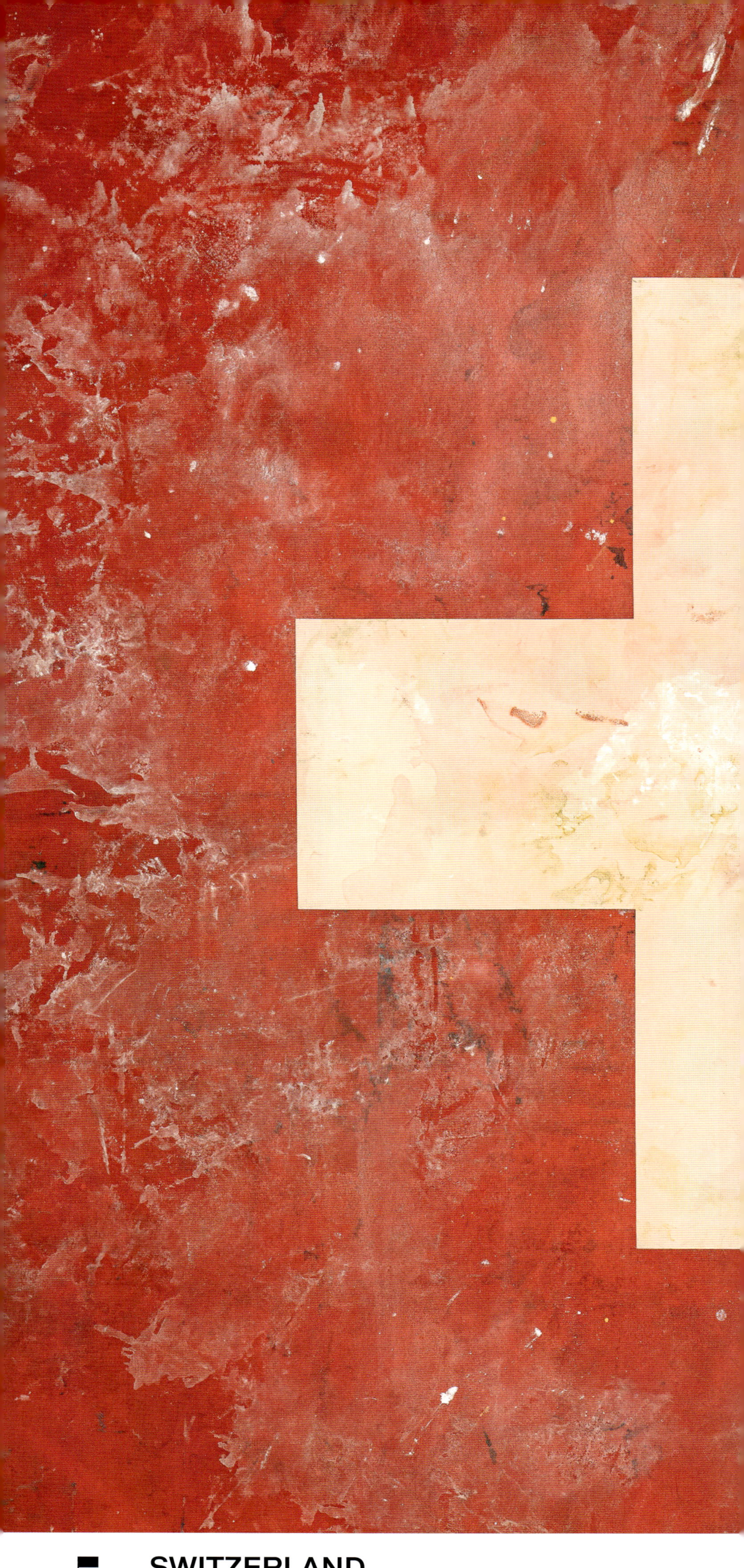

SWITZERLAND

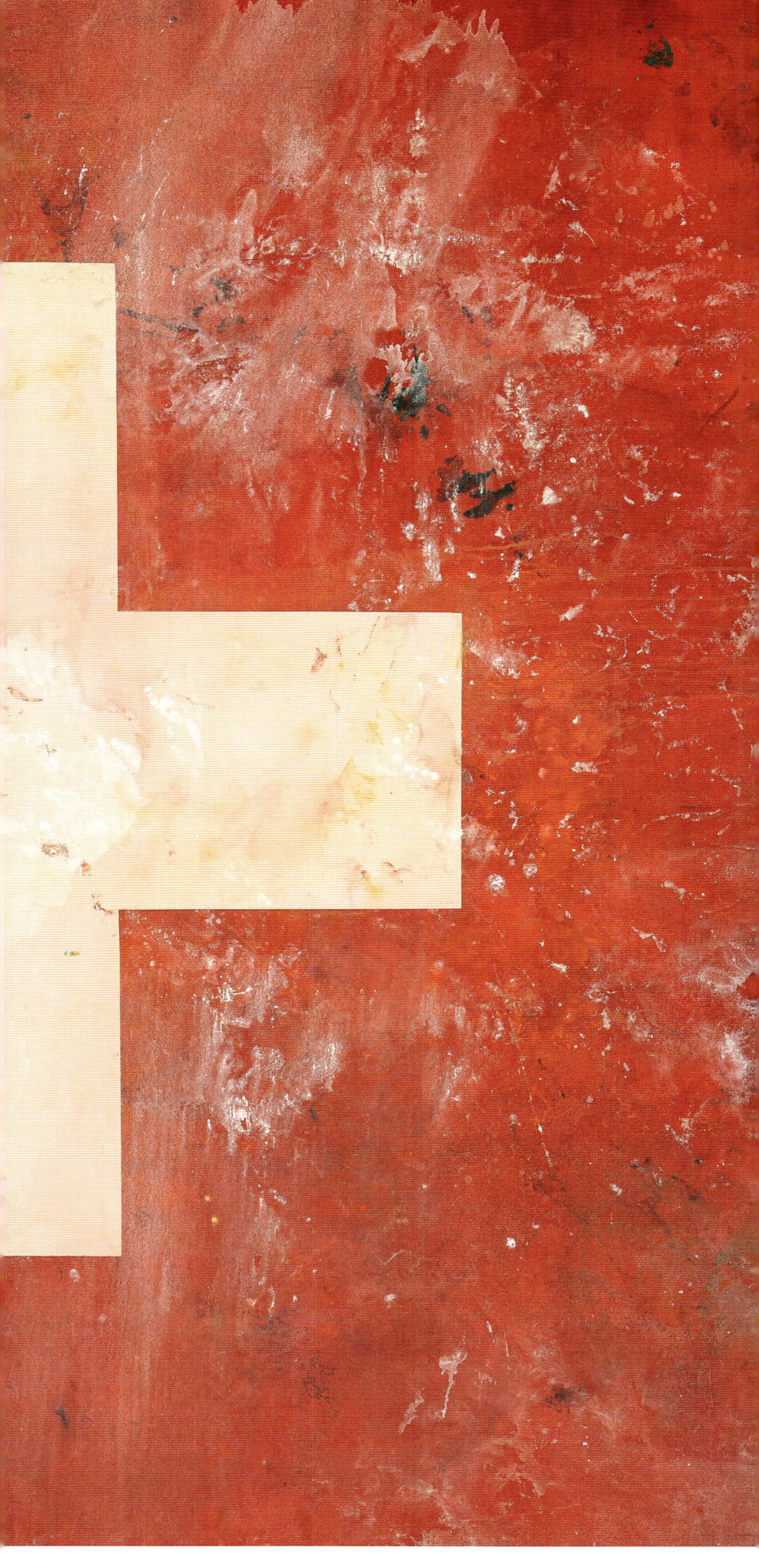

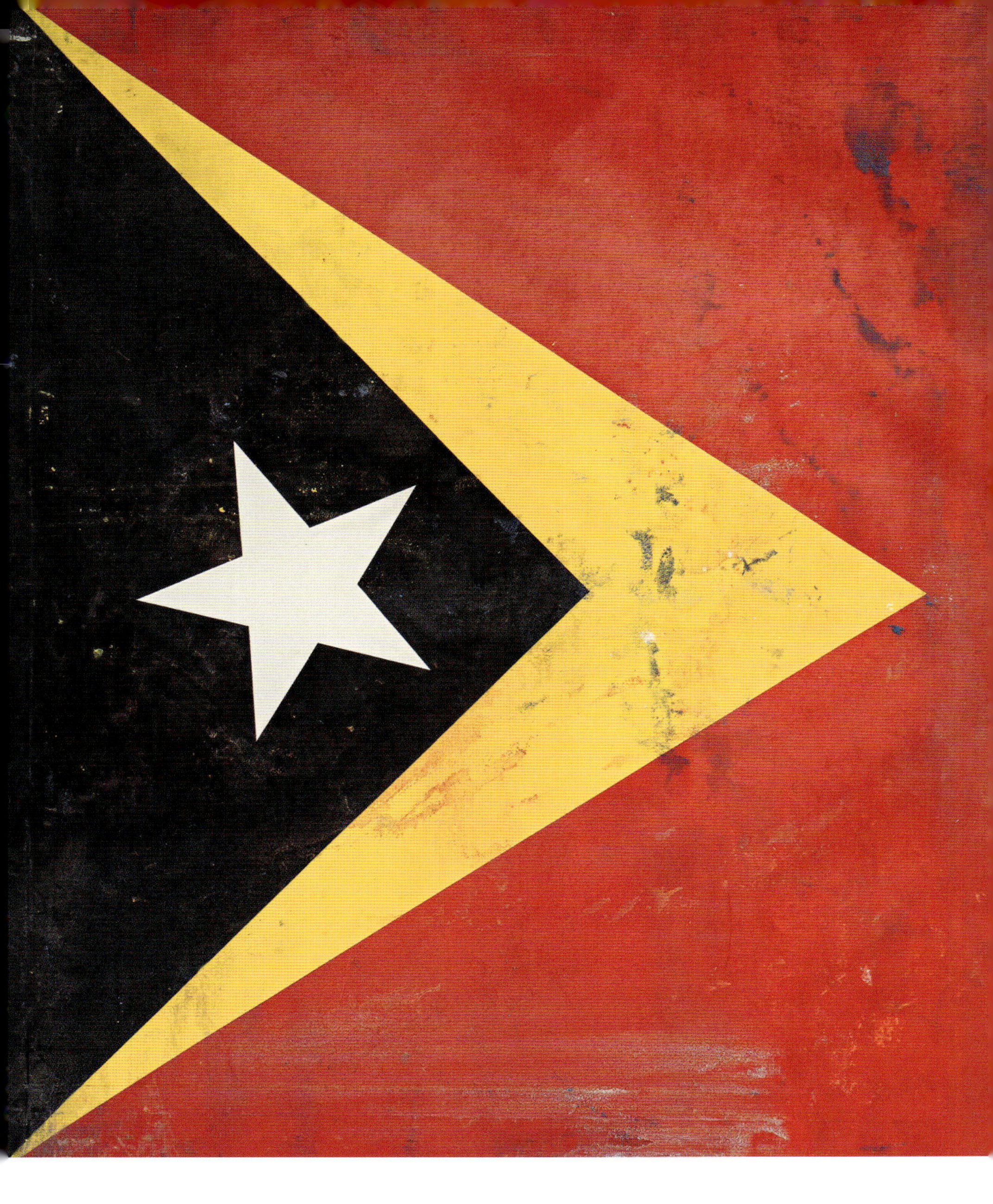

TIMOR-LESTE

P 106

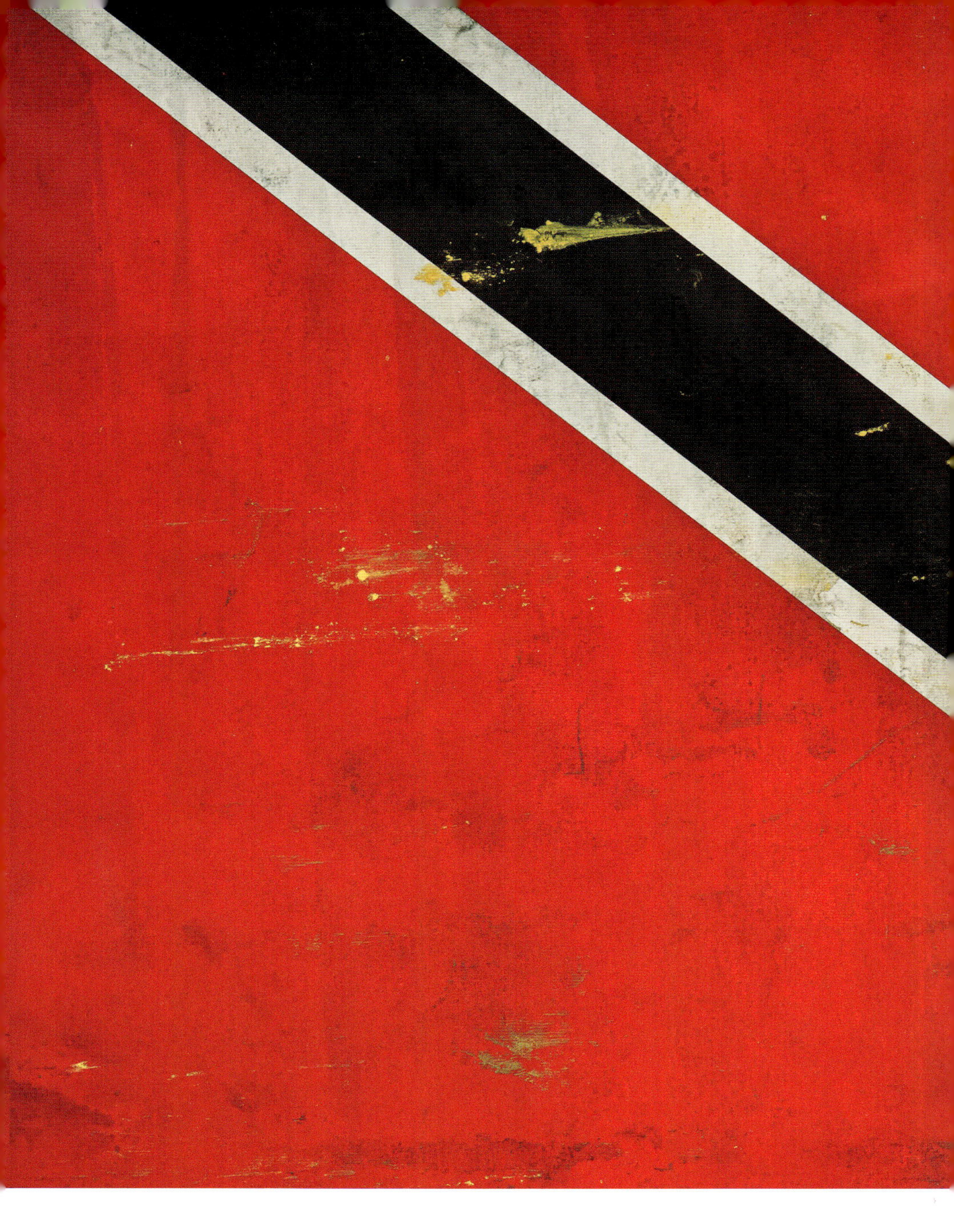

TRINIDAD AND TOBAGO

P 108

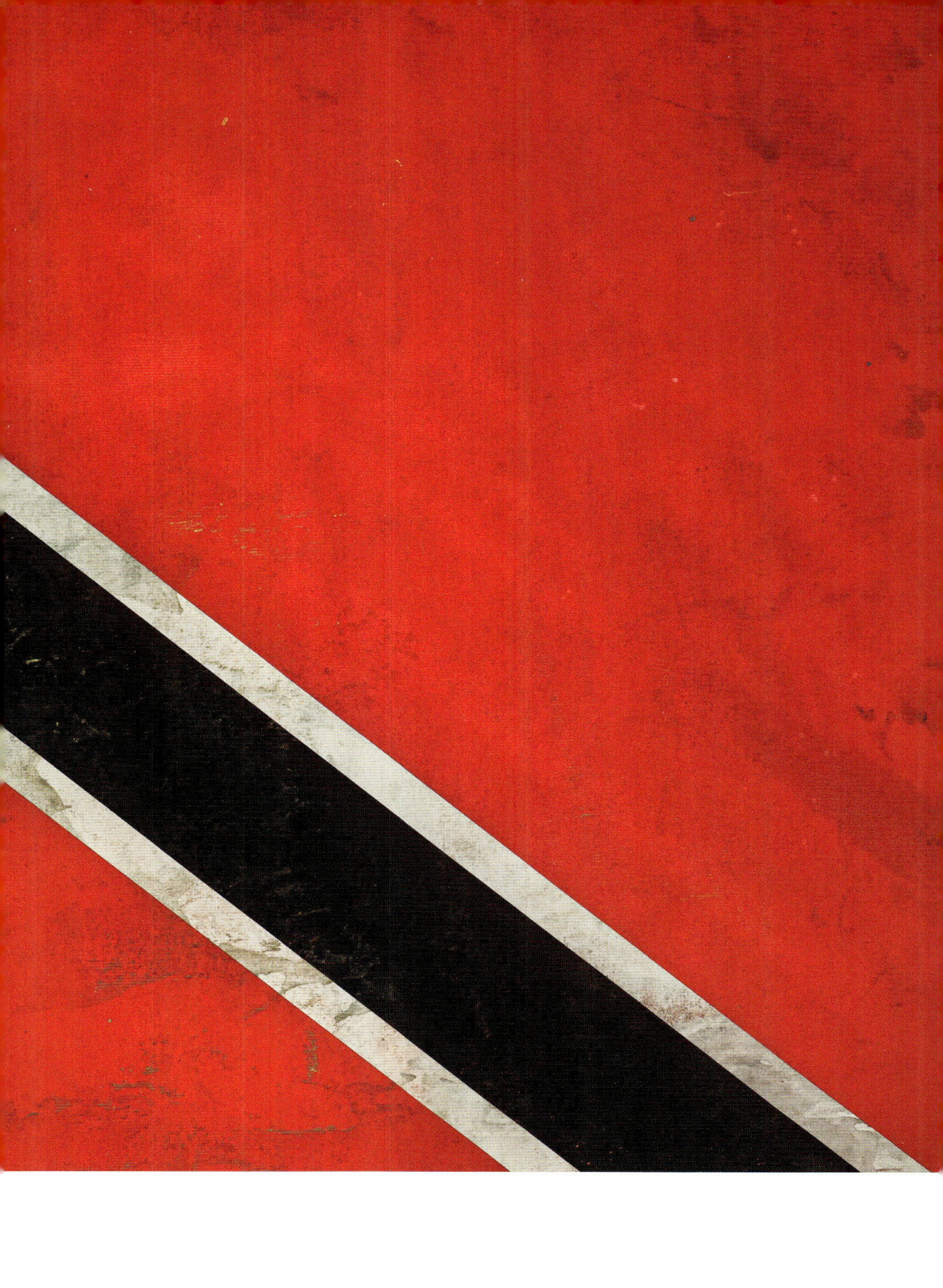

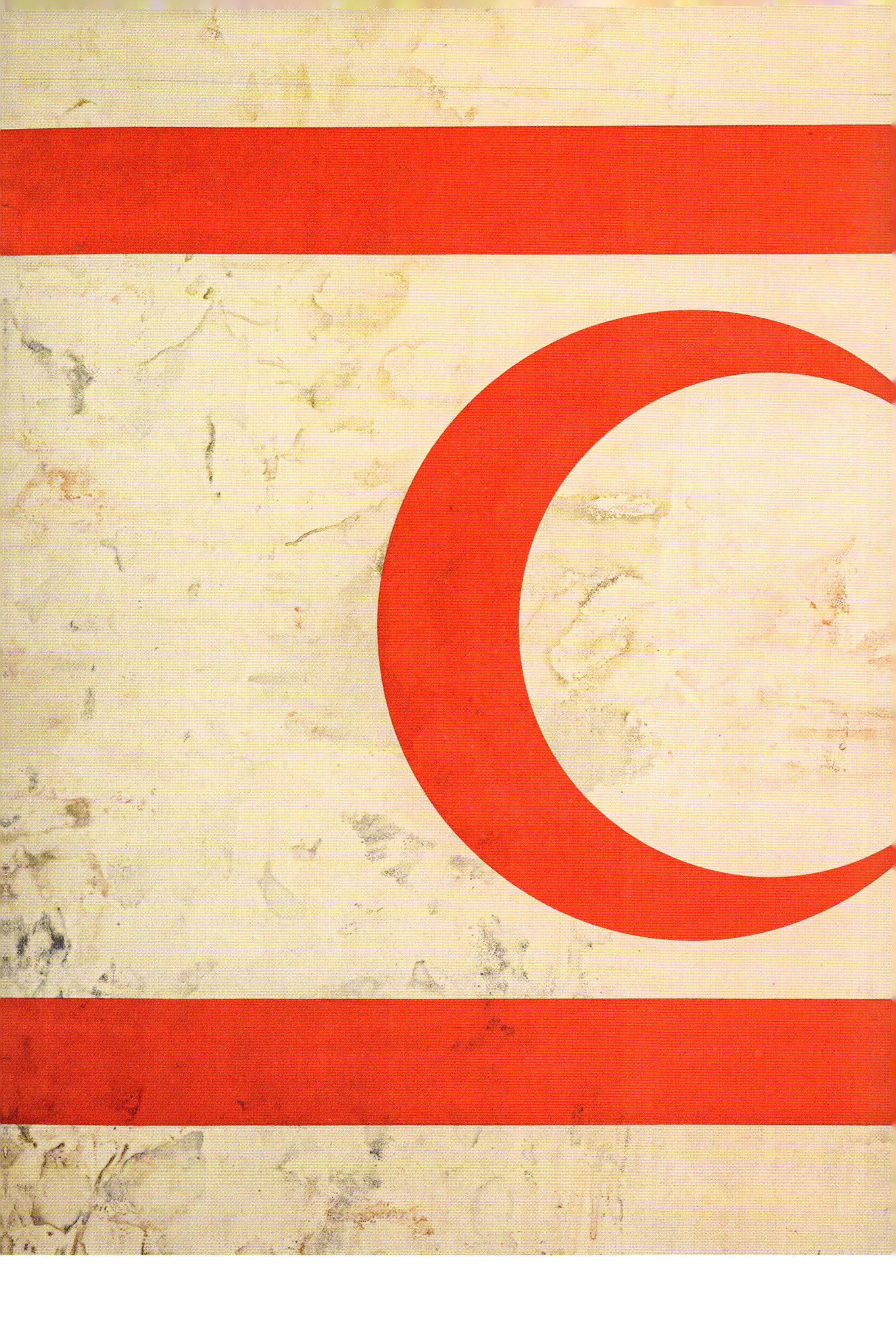

TURKISH REPUBLIC
OF NORTHERN CYPRUS

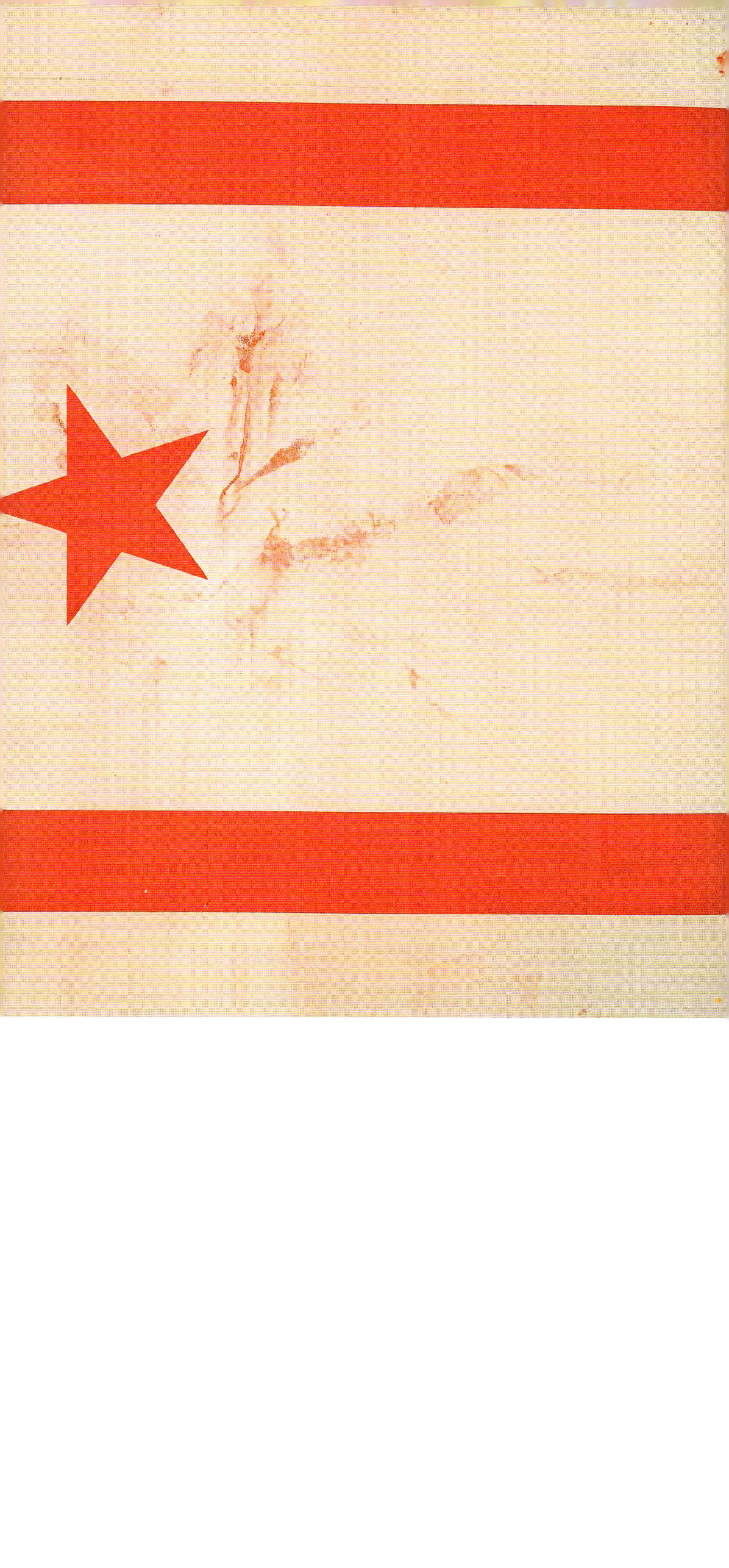

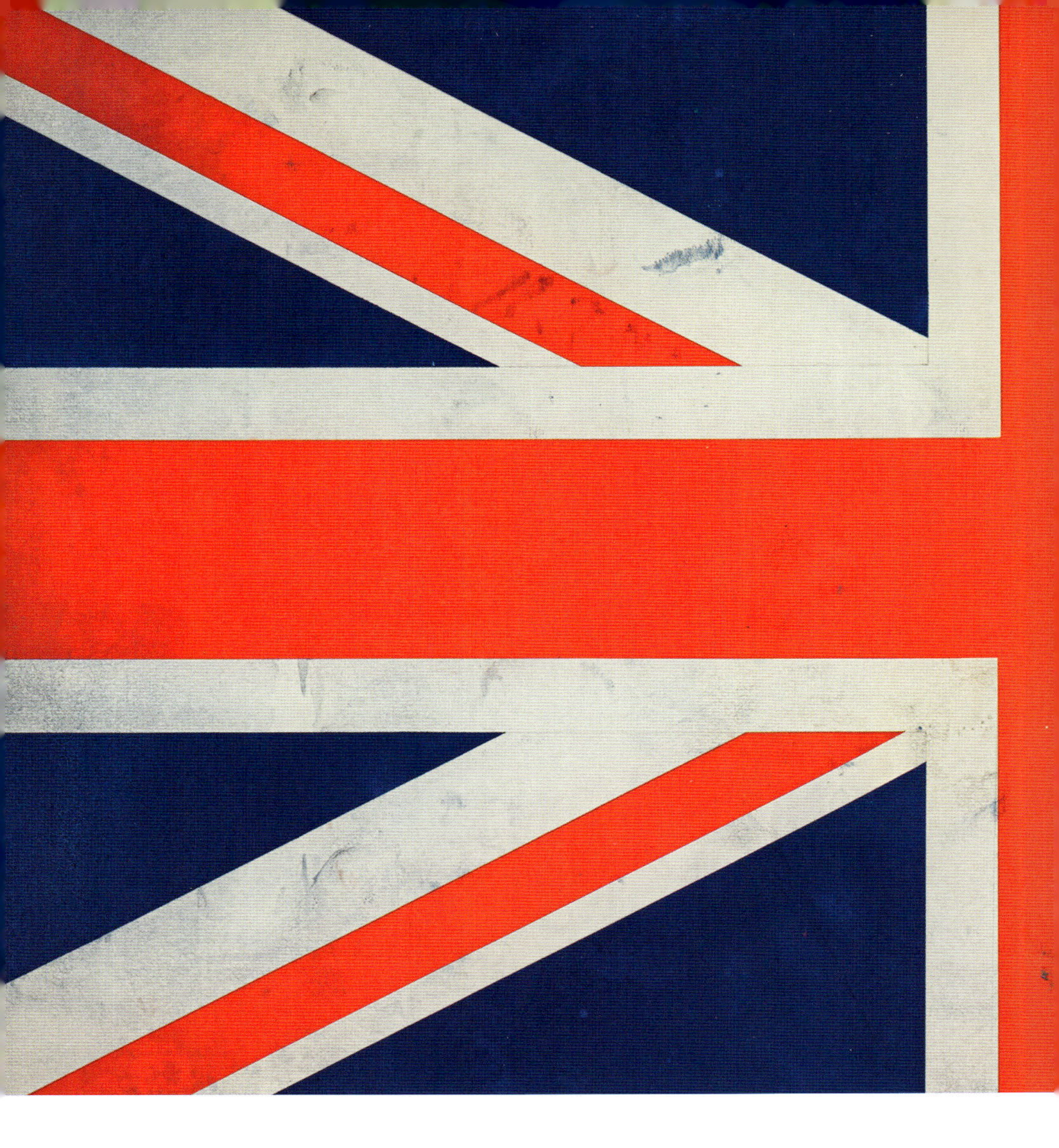

UNITED KINGDOM

P 112

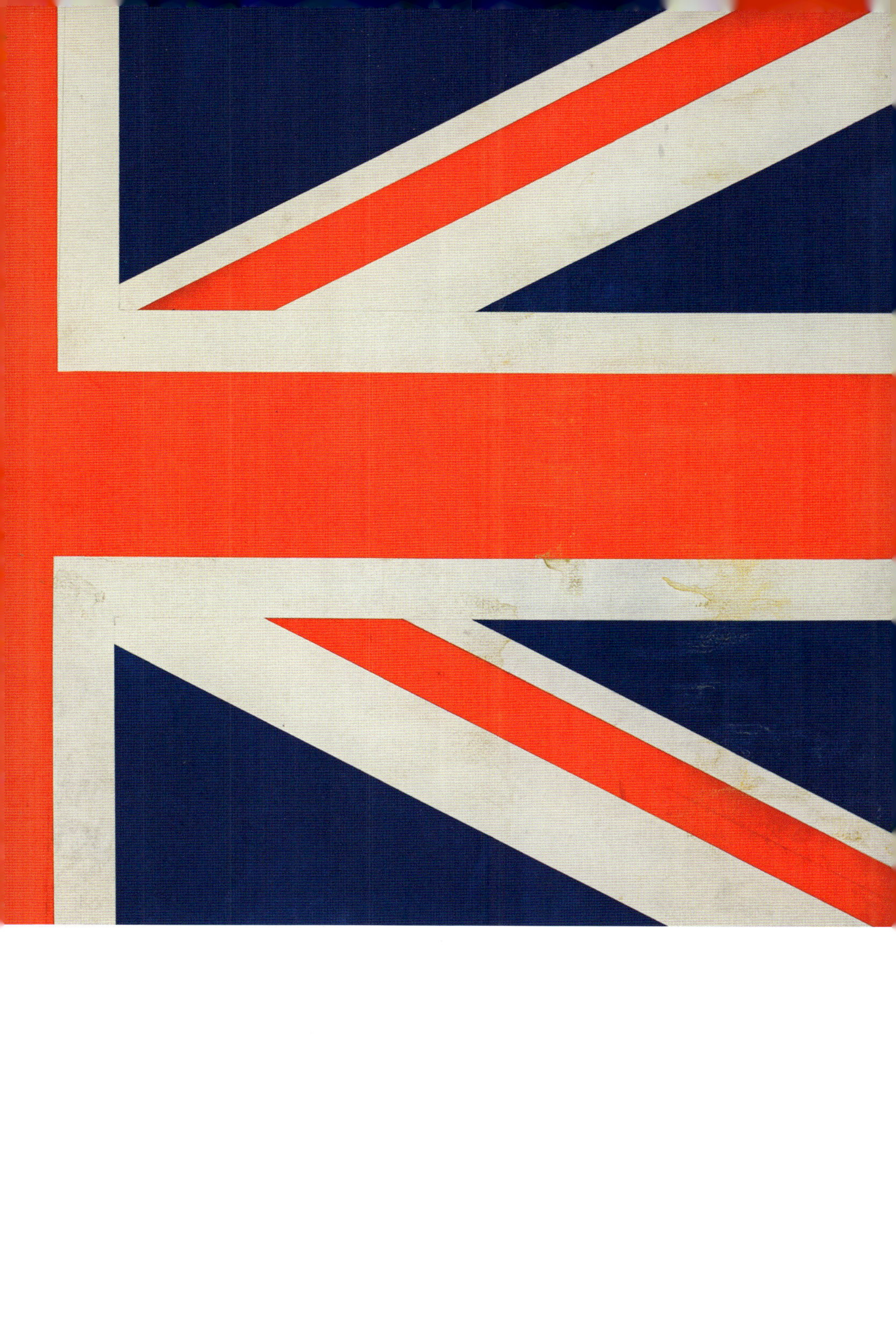

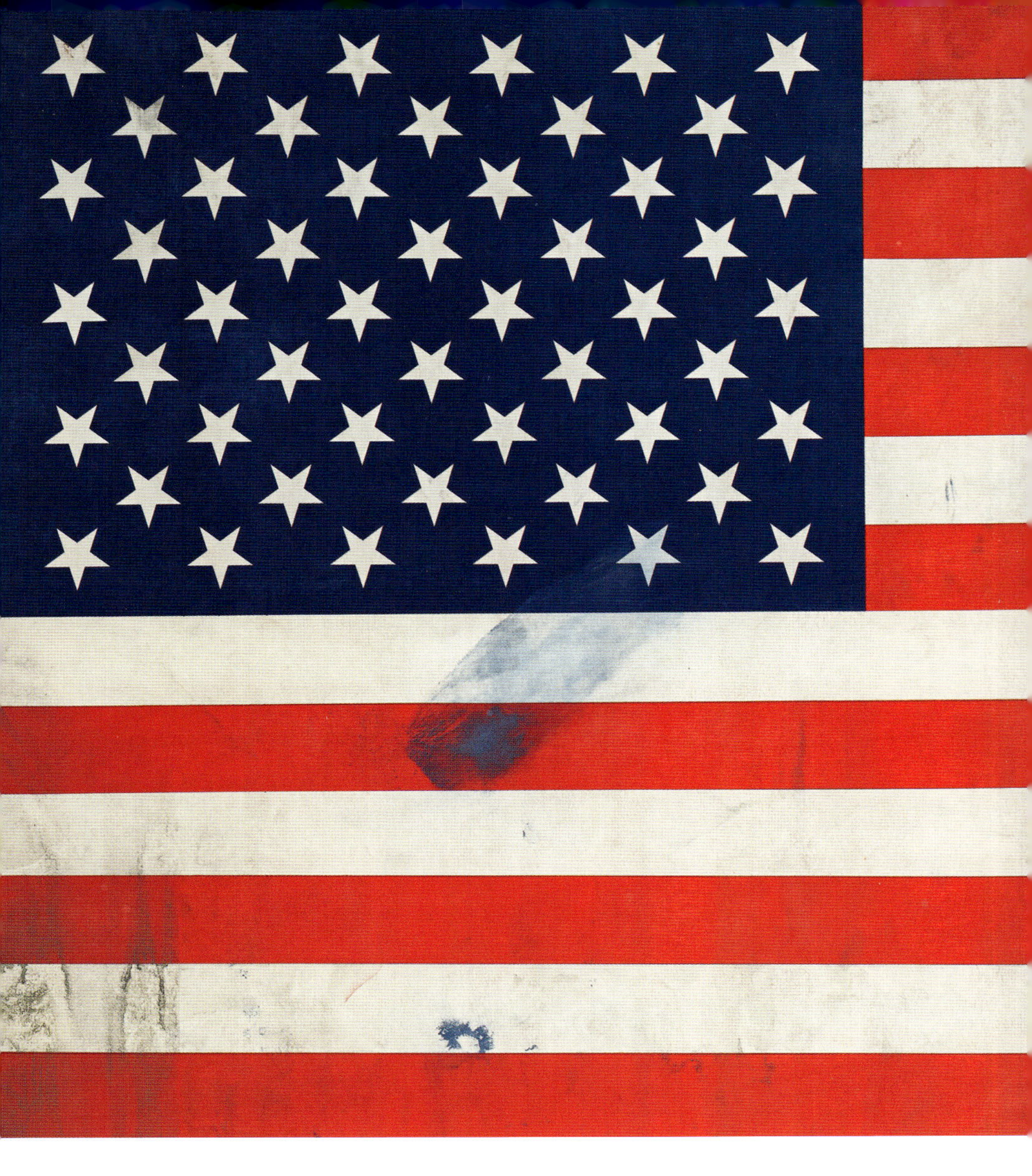

UNITED STATES OF AMERICA

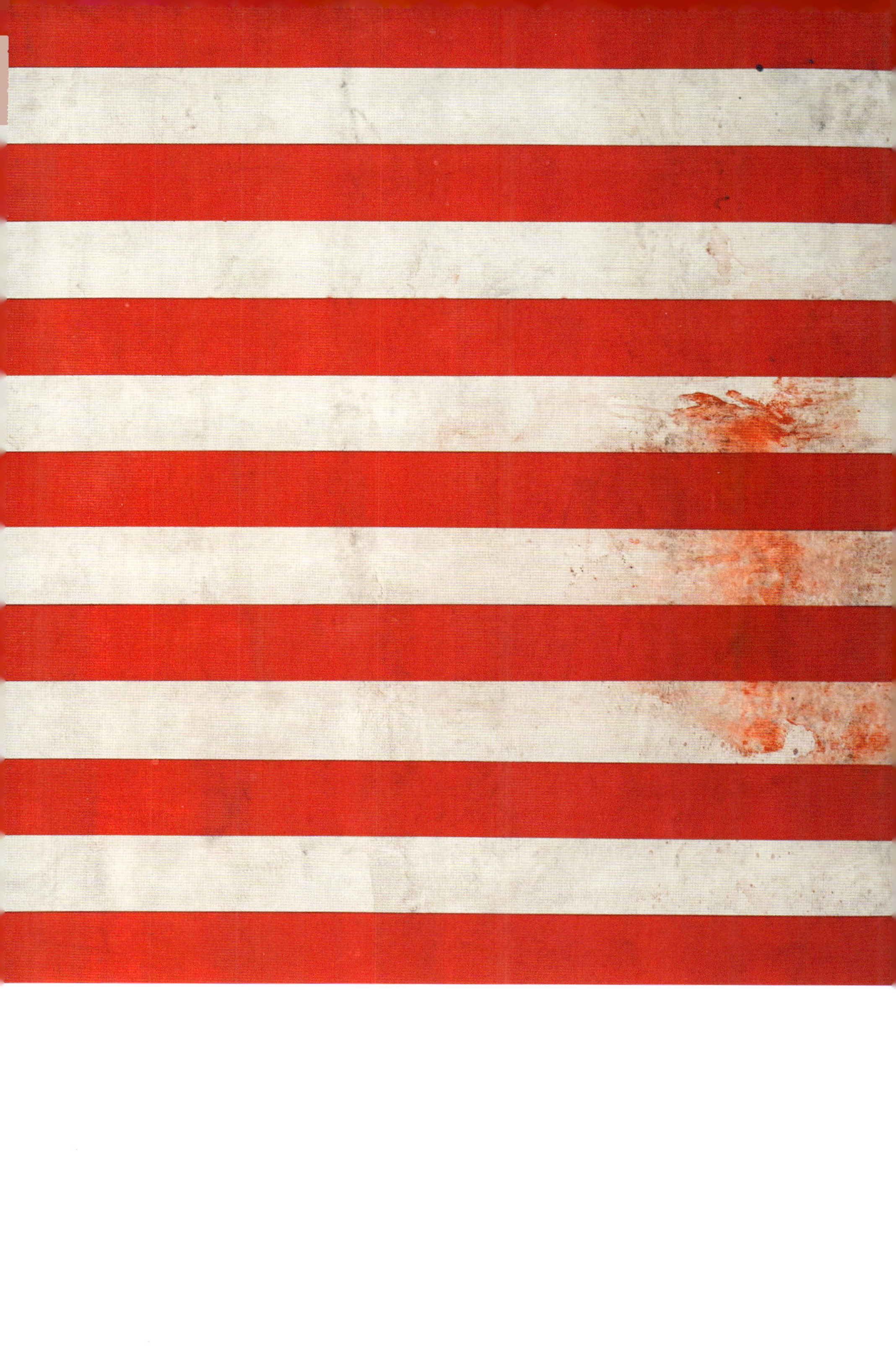

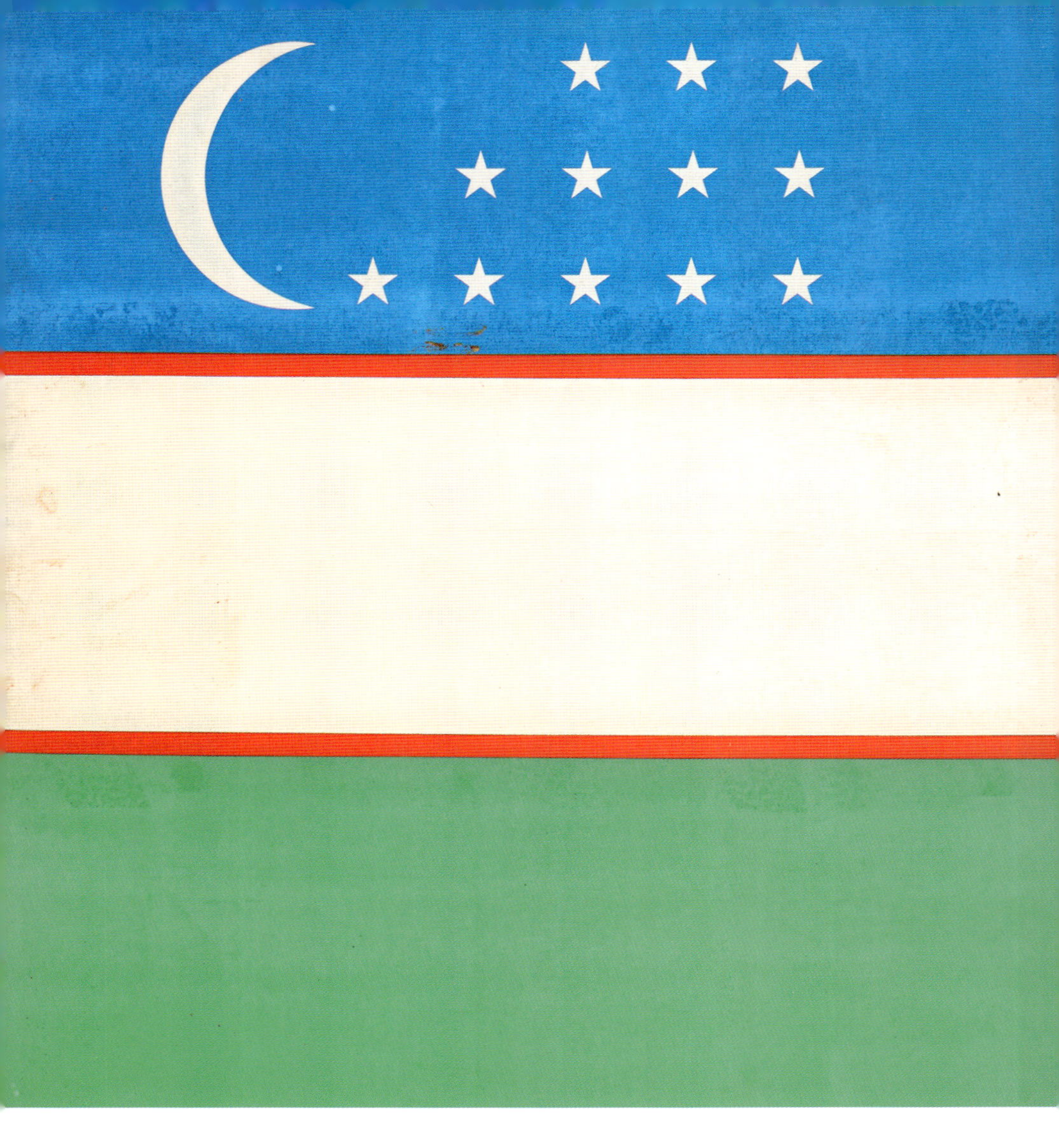

UZBEKISTAN

P 116

AUSTRIA
2019
Spray paint and turpentine on cotton canvas / wooden stretcher
153.5 × 230 × 3.5 cm

BAHRAIN
2020
Spray paint and turpentine on cotton canvas / wooden stretcher
138 × 230 × 3.5 cm

BELARUS
2020
Spray paint and turpentine on cotton canvas / wooden stretcher
115 × 230 × 3.5 cm

BOSNIA AND HERZEGOVINA
2020
Spray paint and turpentine on cotton canvas / wooden stretcher
115 × 230 × 3.5 cm

BOTSWANA
2020
Spray paint and turpentine on cotton canvas / wooden stretcher
153.5 × 230 × 3.5 cm

CANADA
2020
Spray paint and turpentine on cotton canvas / wooden stretcher
115 × 230 × 3.5 cm

CENTRAL AFRICAN REPUBLIC
2020
Spray paint and turpentine on cotton canvas / wooden stretcher
153.5 × 230 × 3.5 cm

CUBA
2020
Spray paint and turpentine on cotton canvas / wooden stretcher
115 × 230 × 3.5 cm

CYPRUS
2020
Spray paint and turpentine on cotton canvas / wooden stretcher
153.5 × 230 × 3.5 cm

CZECH REPUBLIC
2020
Spray paint and turpentine on cotton canvas / wooden stretcher
153.5 × 230 × 3.5 cm

DJIBOUTI
2020
Spray paint and turpentine on cotton canvas / wooden stretcher
153.5 × 230 × 3.5 cm

EGYPT
2020
Spray paint and turpentine on cotton canvas / wooden stretcher
153.5 × 230 × 3.5 cm

ENGLAND
2019
Spray paint and turpentine on cotton canvas / wooden stretcher
138 × 230 × 3.5 cm

FAROE ISLANDS
2020
Spray paint and turpentine on cotton canvas / wooden stretcher
167.2 × 230 × 3.5 cm

FINLAND
2020
Spray paint and turpentine on cotton canvas / wooden stretcher
140.5 × 230 × 3.5 cm

FRANCE
2019
Spray paint and turpentine on cotton canvas / wooden stretcher
153.5 × 230 × 3.5 cm

GEORGIA
2020
Spray paint and turpentine on cotton canvas / wooden stretcher
153.5 × 230 × 3.5 cm

GREECE
2019
Spray paint and turpentine on cotton canvas / wooden stretcher
153.5 × 230 × 3.5 cm

HONDURAS
2020
Spray paint and turpentine on cotton canvas / wooden stretcher
138 × 230 × 3.5 cm

INDIA
2020
Spray paint and turpentine on cotton canvas / wooden stretcher
153.5 × 230 × 3.5 cm

ISRAEL
2020
Spray paint and turpentine on cotton canvas / wooden stretcher
167.2 × 230 × 3.5 cm

ITALY
2019
Spray paint and turpentine on cotton canvas / wooden stretcher
153.5 × 230 × 3.5 cm

JAPAN
2020
Spray paint and turpentine on cotton canvas / wooden stretcher
153.5 × 230 × 3.5 cm

LATVIA
2020
Spray paint and turpentine on cotton canvas / wooden stretcher
115 × 230 × 3.5 cm

LEBANON
2020
Spray paint and turpentine on cotton canvas / wooden stretcher
153.5 × 230 × 3.5 cm

LIBERIA
2020
Spray paint and turpentine on cotton canvas / wooden stretcher
121 × 230 × 3.5 cm

MARSHALL ISLANDS
2020
Spray paint and turpentine on cotton canvas / wooden stretcher
121 × 230 × 3.5 cm

MICRONESIA
2020
Spray paint and turpentine on cotton canvas / wooden stretcher
121 × 230 × 3.5 cm

NAURU
2020
Spray paint and turpentine on cotton canvas / wooden stretcher
115 × 230 × 3.5 cm

NIGERIA
2020
Spray paint and turpentine on cotton canvas / wooden stretcher
115 × 230 × 3.5 cm

NORWAY
2020
Spray paint and turpentine on cotton canvas / wooden stretcher
167.2 × 230 × 3.5 cm

PAKISTAN
2020
Spray paint and turpentine on cotton canvas / wooden stretcher
153.5 × 230 × 3.5 cm

PALESTINE
2020
Spray paint and turpentine on cotton canvas / wooden stretcher
115 × 230 × 3.5 cm

PANAMA
2020
Spray paint and turpentine on cotton canvas / woode stretcher
153.5 × 230 × 3.5 cm

SAINT LUCIA
2020
Spray paint and turpentine on cotton canvas / wooden stretcher
115 × 230 × 3.5 cm

SCOTLAND
2020
Spray paint and turpentine on cotton canvas / wooden stretcher
138 × 230 × 3.5 cm

SEYCHELLES
2020
Spray paint and turpentine on cotton canvas / wooden stretcher
115 × 230 × 3.5 cm

SOUTH AFRICA
2020
Spray paint and turpentine on cotton canvas / wooden stretcher
153.5 × 230 × 3.5 cm

SWITZERLAND
2020
Spray paint and turpentine on cotton canvas / wooden stretcher
230 × 230 × 3.5 cm

TIMOR-LESTE
2020
Spray paint and turpentine on cotton canvas / wooden stretcher
115 × 230 × 3.5 cm

TRINIDAD AND TOBAGO
2020
Spray paint and turpentine on cotton canvas / wooden stretcher
138 × 230 × 3.5 cm

TURKISH REPUBLIC OF NORTHERN CYPRUS
2020
Spray paint and turpentine on cotton canvas / wooden stretcher
153.5 × 230 × 3.5 cm

UNITED KINGDOM
2020
Spray paint and turpentine on cotton canvas / wooden stretcher
115 × 230 × 3.5 cm

UNITED STATES OF AMERICA
2020
Spray paint and turpentine on cotton canvas / wooden stretcher
121 × 230 × 3.5 cm

UZBEKISTAN
2020
Spray paint and turpentine on cotton canvas / wooden stretcher
115 × 230 × 3.5 cm

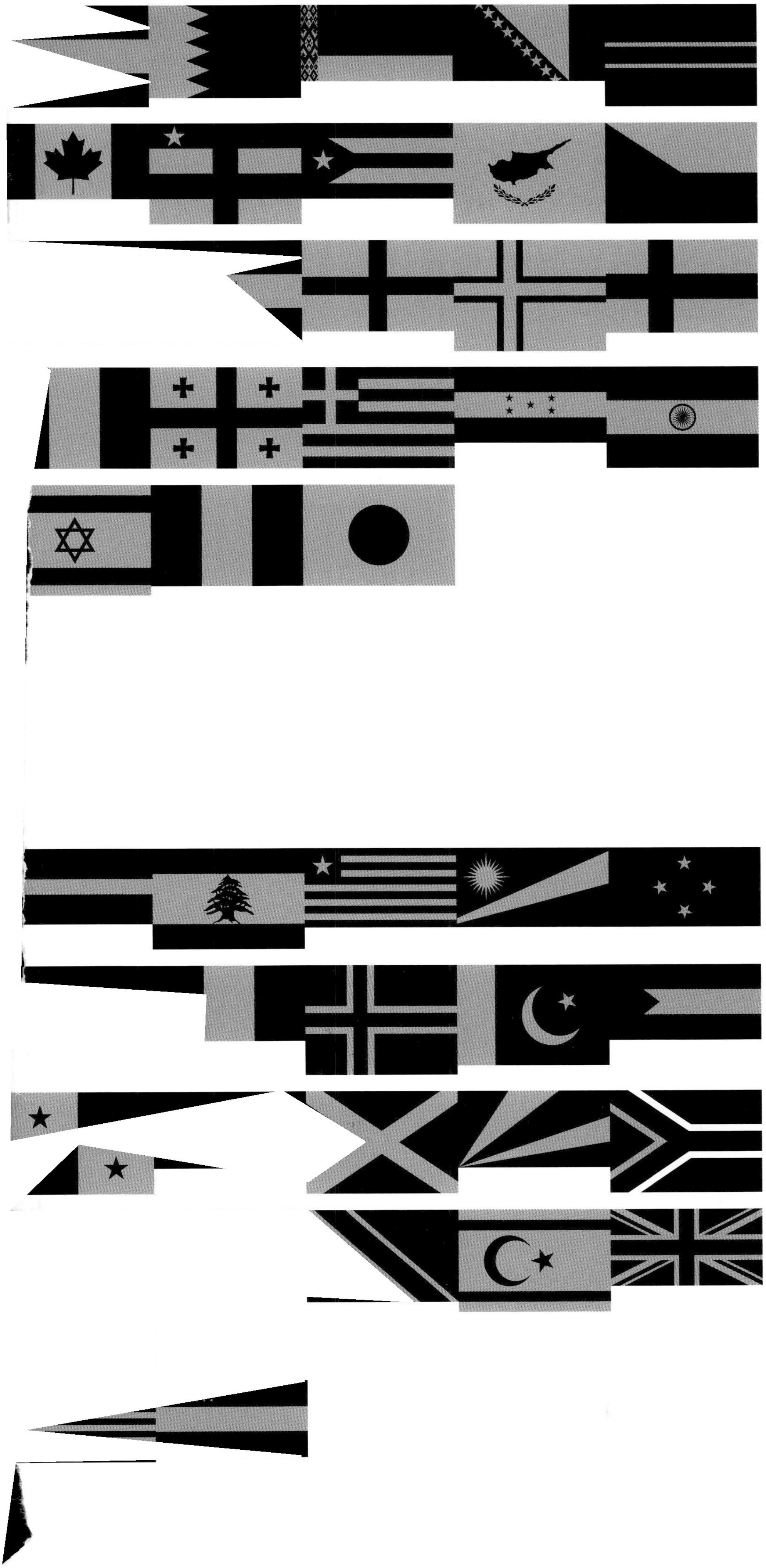

Fredrik Værslev: World Paintings

Essay by:
Dieter Roelstraete

Publishing editor:
Isabella Zamboni—Mousse

Editorial coordination:
Agnese Cantelmi—Mousse

Copyediting:
Lindsey Westbrook

Graphic design:
Francesco Valtolina—Mousse

Design assistance:
Davide Somaschini

Photographs:
Vegard Kleven (pp. 2–46, 74–116)

With the support of Gió Marconi

Published and distributed by
Mousse Publishing
Contrappunto s.r.l.
Corso di Porta Romana 63
20122, Milan–Italy

Available through:

Mousse Publishing, Milan
moussepublishing.com

DAP | Distributed Art Publishers, New York
artbook.com

Vice Versa Distribution, Berlin
viceversaartbooks.com

Les presses du réel, Dijon
lespressesdureel.com

Antenne Books, London
antennebooks.com

First edition: 2020

Printed in Italy by Tipografia Valdostana S.r.l.

ISBN 978-88-6749-447-7

EUR 25 / USD 29.95